CONTENTS

P9-EDV-648

TO THE LEARNER

Building a Strong Vocabulary for Life Skills

This book will help you build your vocabulary and the vocabulary skills you use every day.

*This is a list of the topics in the book. Do you ever talk or read about these things?
Check YES or NO.*

YES	NO	
		Developing learning skills
		Communicating with others
		Finding a place to live
		Getting around town
		Finding a job
		Banking
		Paying for purchases
		Visiting a doctor
		Shopping for healthy food
		Protecting personal information online
		Getting the news
		Being a good citizen

As you work through this book, you will learn many ways to recognize, understand, and use words about these important topics.

About *Building a Strong Vocabulary for Life Skills*

THE UNITS

There are 12 units in this book. Each unit begins with a reading that has 12 vocabulary words. You'll see those words throughout the unit. You'll get lots of practice defining and using them.

VOCABULARY STRATEGIES

You'll also learn strategies you can use to build your vocabulary. These strategies will improve your overall reading and writing skills. And that will help you at home, in your community, at work, and at school.

Word Parts

You will learn about breaking words into parts, including prefixes, suffixes, and roots. When you know the meanings of a word's parts, you can often figure out what the whole word means. You will also learn many compound words and how to work out their meanings.

Context

Did you know that there are clues in most readings that can help you figure out new words? They are called context clues. You will learn how to look for different kinds of clues, such as synonyms, antonyms, examples, and definitions. You will also practice using the clues to work out what a word means.

Dictionary and Parts of Speech

A dictionary is a great resource when you want to build your vocabulary. You can use a dictionary to find out how a word is pronounced, to understand what parts of speech a word can play, and to learn a word's meanings. Many activities in this book will ask you to use a dictionary. The dictionary will help you to understand different parts of speech and to choose the correct meaning of a word.

Multiple Meanings

Many words in English can have more than one meaning. You will practice figuring out the correct meanings of words that you read by thinking about their contexts and how the words are used in sentences.

FEATURES

Exercises

Practice is the best way to learn something new. So each unit has lots of activities that will help you learn new words and try new vocabulary strategies. The more you do, the more you'll remember. Studies show that people learn new words when they see them several times and practice using them in different ways.

Tips

Tips appear on the sides of many pages. You'll find helpful hints there. Some tips give information about specific words, such as how to say or spell them. Others describe strategies that you can use to figure out word meanings. Read the tips before you do the exercises. They can help you complete the work and develop your vocabulary skills.

Personalization Activities

Many pages include questions for you to answer using your own experiences, ideas, and knowledge. There are no right or wrong answers to these questions. Asking and answering personal questions is an excellent way to practice and remember new words. You will develop your writing, speaking, and listening skills as you complete these activities.

Answer Key and Word Part Lists

You can check your answers by looking in the Answer Key at the back of this book. You will also find lists of common prefixes, suffixes, and roots there. These lists will be good resources even after you finish the book.

Personal Dictionary

Use the Personal Dictionary on page 112 to keep track of new words you learn.

SETTING GOALS

Many students define their success in school by setting and meeting goals. A goal is something you want to achieve. You may have a goal for using this book. Maybe you want to be a better reader. Maybe you want to get a better job. Maybe you want to pass a test.

Complete this sentence:

I'm using this book because I want to _____

_____

Come back and review this page every few weeks. You may find that you need or want to revise your goal.

1 Developing Learning Skills

VOCABULARY

Read these words from the passage. Check the words you know.

- [ ] active
- [ ] balance
- [ ] commitments
- [ ] connect
- [ ] counselors
- [ ] focus
- [ ] opinions
- [ ] participate
- [ ] reasonable
- [ ] resource
- [ ] stress
- [ ] succeed

"The only person who is educated is the one who has learned how to learn and change." —Carl Rogers

We all know that learning is important, but we don't all know the best way to do it. Here are some skills you can develop to become the best learner you can be.

First, be an **active** learner. Come to class prepared. Pay attention, and use your time well. Let your teacher know you're in the room by asking good questions and giving thoughtful answers. **Participate** in class discussions and be open to other students' **opinions**. You will not always agree with them (and they won't always agree with you), but they might still have something interesting to say.

Think about how what you are hearing or reading about interests you. Try to **connect** what you are learning to things you already know. That will make new information easier for you to understand and remember.

When you're not in class, you'll need to find time to study. It isn't easy to **balance** school and the rest of your life. You already have a lot of **commitments**, including your family. If it feels like there just isn't enough time in a day to get everything done, ask for help. Find the learning or **resource** center at school. **Counselors** are there to help you, and they want the same thing you do: they want you to **succeed**.

When you do find time to study, try to study for about an hour at a time. If you can't **focus**, take time off and do something else. Sometimes a short break is all you need. Try to find a good learning place. Some people like a quiet place to study. Others prefer to be around other people when they study.

It helps to set goals. Your goals should be **reasonable**. They should not add **stress** to your life. A reasonable goal might be to finish your homework by a certain day or time. Setting and reaching small goals will help you reach your larger goals.

Following these suggestions will make you a better and more successful learner. Try them and see.

What are two good reasons for having a special time or place to study?

_____

_____

1. Vocabulary Focus

Match the word with its definition. Write the correct letter.

_____	1. active	a.	a feeling of worry that keeps you from relaxing
_____	2. balance	b.	a promise to do something
_____	3. commitment	c.	to do something together with other people
_____	4. connect	d.	someone who advises
_____	5. counselor	e.	busy and doing a lot of things
_____	6. focus	f.	to achieve something you wanted to do
_____	7. opinion	g.	to concentrate
_____	8. participate	h.	to give things equal importance
_____	9. reasonable	i.	to join one thing or person to another
_____	10. resource	j.	what you think about something
_____	11. stress	k.	a person or thing that can help you
_____	12. succeed	l.	fair or right

Commitment is spelled with a double m and one t.

2. Use the Vocabulary

Write three things you can do to be a more active learner.

1. _____

   _____

2. _____

   _____

3. _____

   _____

Share your answers with a partner. Talk about ideas for revising them and make changes. Then read your answers aloud to the class.

3. Work With New Vocabulary

Write your answers to the questions. Then compare answers with a partner.

1. You will **focus** better in class if you get a good night's sleep. What are two other things you can do before class to stay focused?

   _____

2. Where are the offices of the **counselors** at your school?

   _____

3. How can it help you to listen to people whose **opinions** are different from yours?

   _____

4. How do you **balance** school with the other things you have to do?

   _____

5. What does it mean to you to **succeed**? Make a list of important successes in your life.

   _____

6. Are you an **active** person? What are some things you could do to be more active?

   _____

7. How can you **connect** with other students in your class or at your school?

   _____

8. You can take a walk or a quick shower during a study break. What are three other **reasonable** things you can do to relax or refresh on a study break?

   _____

9. What causes **stress** in your life?

   _____

10. What **resources** are available to you at your school?

    _____

11. Do you need to make a **commitment** if you want to succeed? Explain your answer.

    _____

12. What advice do you have for friends who don't like to **participate** in class?

    _____

4. Prefixes *il-*, *in-*, *im-*, and *ir-*

A prefix is a word part at the beginning of a word. The prefixes *il-*, *in-*, *im-*, and *ir-* mean "not" or "the opposite of." For example, *impolite* means "not polite."

The underlined word in each sentence starts with the prefix il-, in-, im-, or ir-. Write the definition of the underlined word. Use a dictionary to check your answers.

1. Jackie is unhappy with the <u>imbalance</u> in her life. She thinks she spends too much time at school and work and not enough time with her friends and family.

   definition: _____

2. In English, the past tense of most verbs ends in *–ed*. However, verbs with <u>irregular</u> past tense forms don't follow the *–ed* rule.

   definition: _____

   ● Use *ir-* before words that begin with *r*.

3. Ben got two <u>incorrect</u> answers on the history test, but he passed anyway.

   definition: _____

4. It's <u>impossible</u> to find a quiet place to study at home, so I go to the library when I can.

   definition: _____

5. A study group presented its ideas for solving the <u>illegal</u> immigration problem to the rest of the class.

   definition: _____

   ● Use *il-* before words that begin with *l*.

5. Suffix *–ful*

A suffix is a word part at the end of a word. The suffix *–ful* means "full of." You can add *–ful* to the end of some words to make nouns and adjectives.

● The suffix *–ful* is spelled with only one *l*.

Complete the conversations. Use words from the list. Check a dictionary if you don't know the meaning of a word.

meaningful	peaceful	stressful	successful

1. A: Diana just got a new job. She's going to manage the third floor of the hospital.

   B: She's been so _____. You must be very proud of her.

2. A: Why is that ring so _____ to you?

   B: It was my grandmother's ring. She gave it to my mother, and my mother gave it to me. It's been in our family for more than 75 years.

3. A: Are you OK? You don't look well.

   B: It's been a really _____ week. I had to take two tests at school and give a presentation at work. I guess I'm just tired.

4. A: When Lawrence studies, he likes to listen to music.

   B: Not me! I need to be in a quiet, _____ place.

6. Compound Words

You can find many compound words in a dictionary. If you can't find the compound you're looking for, look up each word part separately.

A compound word is made up of two or more other words. Sometimes a compound word is written as one word, as in *textbook*. Sometimes there is a space between the words, as in *high school*. Sometimes a hyphen divides the words, as in *mother-in-law*. To understand the meaning of a compound word, think about the meanings of the words that make up the compound.

Complete the sentences. Use words from the list.

brainstorm	checklist	full-time	online classes	study group

1. Let's _____ a good place for you to study. We'll write down all the places we can think of and see which one you like the best.

2. This year, Vince is taking _____. He enjoys just turning on his computer when he's ready to begin studying, but sometimes it's difficult for him to focus.

3. I have a _____ of more than 20 things I need to do before classes start next week. The only thing I've done so far is buy my books.

4. In addition to studying and going to classes, many adult students have _____ jobs and families to take care of.

5. Have you ever thought of joining a _____? You meet with other students to discuss and review what you're doing in class.

7. Context Clues: Definitions and Synonyms

Words such as *are*, *is*, *means*, *or*, and *refers* often indicate a definition.

If you're trying to figure out an unfamiliar word, look for clues in what comes before and after that word. A context clue may be the definition of the word or it may be a synonym, a word with a similar meaning. Use these clues to figure out the meaning of an unknown word.

Read each sentence. Look for clues to help you understand the meaning of the boldfaced word. Write the meaning of the word on the line.

1. When you set a goal, try to **visualize** the end result. Have a picture of it in your mind.

   To *visualize* means _____

2. Music and noise **distract** me when I'm doing my homework. I need to study in a completely quiet place. Music stops me from thinking about what I'm doing.

   To *distract* means _____

3. Part of your job as a student is to find out what learning resources are **available** to you. Can you go to the library, visit a museum, or search the Web? Find everything that is ready for you to use, have, or see.

   Available means _____

4. Participating actively in class is a great **strategy**, or plan, for meeting your goals.

   A *strategy* is _____

Name one learning strategy you've used to help yourself do well in school.

_____

8. Parts of Speech and the Dictionary

Some words can be used for more than one part of speech. For example, as a noun *focus* can mean "the subject of attention or interest." (*The focus of her talk was student safety.*) As a verb, *focus* can mean "to give all your attention to something or someone." (*I can focus better in a quiet room.*)

Look at the boldfaced words. Are they nouns or verbs? Circle the correct part of speech. Then look up the word in a dictionary. Write the correct definition on the line.

noun   verb   1. If you're tired and can't **form** a clear thought, it's probably time to take a break from studying.

_____

noun   verb   2. The first step in learning is to gather information. Use all of your **senses**—sight, smell, sound, taste, and touch—for help.

_____

noun   verb   3. **Review** your work before you give it to your teacher. It's always a good idea to think about something again to see if it needs to be changed.

_____

noun   verb   4. **Record** new ideas in a journal. Write down the things that you want to remember and the questions you want to ask.

_____

> ● When you look up a word in the dictionary, make sure you are looking at the correct part of speech.
>
> n = noun
> v = verb
> adj = adjective
> adv = adverb
> prep = preposition

> ● When the word *record* is a noun, say RECord. When *record* is a verb, say reCORD.

9. Multiple-Meaning Words

Some words have more than one meaning. To find the right meaning, look at how the word is used in the sentence. You can also look at nearby words for clues.

Look at the underlined word. Circle the letter of the best definition.

1. Write down important information right away. If you let too much time <u>pass</u>, it will be harder to remember.
   a. to go by
   b. to complete a test or exam successfully

2. I can't study for a long <u>period</u>. I get tired and bored.
   a. a mark you use at the end of a sentence
   b. an amount of time

3. What does it <u>mean</u> to be an active learner?
   a. imply
   b. unkind

4. I can't <u>stress</u> enough how much I want to find a quiet place to study.
   a. to say something strongly to show that it is important
   b. to feel worried and unable to relax

Unit 1 Review

Complete the paragraphs. Use words from the lists.

active	balance	commitment	counselor	resource	stress	succeed

Leila was excited when she went back to school last year, but the experience was not what she had expected. She found it difficult to (1) _____ school and the rest of her life. She thought she couldn't go to school and take care of herself and her family.

After her first week of classes, Leila decided to talk to her (2) _____, Martin, at the student center. She told Martin that she was unhappy about the (3) _____ that school was adding to her life. She worried that she couldn't be an (4) _____ student and a good mother, wife, and daughter. Martin told Leila that things would get easier in a few weeks. He reminded her of her strong (5) _____ to her education and her future.

Two weeks later, Leila met with Martin again. She said she was feeling better and thanked him for his support. He said he'd always believed that Leila would (6) _____ and that she could talk to him again any time. Martin's been a great (7) _____ for Leila and other students who ask him for advice.

connect	focus	opinion	participate	reasonable

Ms. James, the director of our school, spoke to us about how to act like a good student. First, she said that if you want to be a good student, you have to (8) _____ on what is going on in class. If you listen carefully and (9) _____ in group discussions and other activities, your teachers will notice and think of you as a good student. In my (10) _____, that makes a lot of sense, but it isn't always easy. Sometimes when I'm in class, I start thinking about what's going on at work, what I'm going to have for dinner, or when I can get to the bank. . .

Ms. James also said to try to (11) _____ the information in the lesson to what you already know. She said that makes it easier to understand and remember. If you're having trouble, ask for help. She said this will show your teacher you're interested in what's going on. I know that asking for help is a (12) _____ thing to do, but it's also the most difficult one for me.

Read each question. Then circle the correct answer.

1. **Which definition of *balance* matches the meaning in this sentence?**

   Mae and her friends talked about the importance of finding <u>balance</u> in their lives.

   A A state in which two or more things have the proper amount of importance

   B to make two things equal

   C the ability to keep steady

   D an amount of money in a bank account

2. **What does the word *connect* mean in this passage?**

   Some of what you learn is based on what you have already learned. A good way to remember new ideas is to <u>connect</u> them to what you know.

   A to join a computer or a mobile device to the Internet or to a computer network

   B to fasten one thing to another

   C to join two or more thoughts

   D to form a good relationship with somebody you like and understand

3. **Which of these words means "full of meaning"?**

   A meaningless

   B meaner

   C meaningful

   D meanly

4. **Which of these words is the opposite of *expensive*?**

   A expenses

   B expensively

   C expensiveness

   D inexpensive

5. **What does the word *resources* mean in this sentence?**

   Of all the <u>resources</u> available at school, I think I use the library and the computer lab most often.

   A help

   B money

   C ability

   D staff

6. **Which definition of *reasonable* best matches the meaning in this sentence?**

   Catherine thought it was <u>reasonable</u> to work full time during the week and go to school on Saturdays.

   A practical; sensible

   B fairly good

   C affordable; not too expensive

   D fair

7. **Which word from the passage means about the same as *focus*?**

   Danny always sat in the middle seat of the front row in class. He would concentrate on what the teacher was saying to be sure he understood everything. He tried to answer every question. His goal was to be the best student in the class.

   A middle

   B concentrate

   C tried

   D goal

8. **Which of these sentences means that Roy's homework was *incomplete*?**

   A Roy finished his homework.

   B Roy did some of his homework.

   C Roy got help with his homework.

   D Roy didn't have any homework.

What advice would you give a new student at your school? Write your answer on a separate sheet of paper. Use at least six words you learned in this unit. Circle the vocabulary words you use.

Check your answers on page 104.

2 Communicating With Others

VOCABULARY

Read these words from the passage. Check the words you know.

- ☐ appreciate
- ☐ communication
- ☐ confident
- ☐ cooperate
- ☐ effective
- ☐ improve
- ☐ key
- ☐ message
- ☐ perspective
- ☐ react
- ☐ research
- ☐ skills

There are many forms of communication, and more than one kind of communication can take place at one time. The goal of all communication is understanding.

Research shows that most success in life is connected to good **communication**. Communication is the process of sharing information, ideas, or feelings. Communication is **effective** when both the sender and the receiver understand the same information.

Good communication is **key** to meeting goals at work, at home, and in school. Unfortunately, sometimes there are misunderstandings. The meaning of a **message** can get lost between the thought and the act of communicating it. That's why it's important to develop good communication **skills**. The more you **improve** your ability to send and receive information, the more successful you will be.

Make eye contact when you speak. When you look people in the eye, it tells them that you are **confident** in yourself and in your message. People will pay more attention to you. However, too much eye contact can make people uncomfortable, so look away every once in a while.

Be aware of your body language. Your body can sometimes say more than words do. For example, if your arms are crossed, you may look closed off. If your arms are by your side or open, you look open and interested. People **react** to body language even if they aren't aware of it at the time.

Learn to listen. Communication is a two-way street. Focus on what the other person has to say, not on what you're going to say next. Speak in a way that lets them know you care about what they have to say. People **appreciate** it when you try to understand their **perspectives**, or points of view. They are more likely to want to work and **cooperate** with you.

Do you know any other words about being a good communicator? Write them here.

_____ _____ _____

1. Vocabulary Focus

Match the word with its definition. Write the correct letter.

_____ 1. appreciate   a. to make better

_____ 2. communication   b. information that you give to a person

_____ 3. confident   c. things you can do well

_____ 4. cooperate   d. to say or do something because something has happened

_____ 5. effective   e. sharing information, feelings, or ideas

_____ 6. improve   f. your way of thinking about something

_____ 7. key   g. important

_____ 8. message   h. to work together with someone else in a helpful way

_____ 9. perspective   i. the study of something to find out more about it

_____ 10. react   j. sure of yourself

_____ 11. research   k. to value

_____ 12. skills   l. likely to succeed

2. Use the Vocabulary

Write about someone you think is an effective communicator. The person can be a friend, a family member, or someone you've heard speak online, on TV, or on the radio. Use at least three words from the vocabulary list. Underline the vocabulary words you use.

_____

_____

_____

_____

_____

3. Work With New Vocabulary

Write your answers. Then compare answers with a partner.

1. What are two things that have been **key** to your success at work or at school?

   _____

2. How can you let a person you are talking with know that you are interested in his **perspective**?

   _____

3. What are three **effective** ways of getting people's attention?

   _____

4. Who is the most difficult person for you to **communicate** with? Why?

   _____

5. How do you usually let friends know that you **appreciate** something they've done for you?

   _____

6. What is the most important **skill** you need to be a good writer? Explain your answer.

   _____

7. Why do you think it's important to seem **confident** when you speak to a group of people?

   _____

8. Describe **research** you've done for school, your job, or your family.

   _____

9. What are two things you'd like to **improve** about yourself?

   _____

10. How do you **react** when a friend doesn't agree with you? What about when your boss doesn't agree with you?

    _____

11. What are some ways you can **cooperate** with other students in your class?

    _____

12. Do you prefer to share personal **messages** with friends by texting, by email, by phone, or in person? Why?

    _____

4. Prefix *mis–*

The prefix *mis–* means "wrong" or "wrongly." You can usually figure out the word's meaning when a word begins with the prefix *mis–*. For example, *miscommunicated* means "communicated wrongly."

The prefix *mis–* can be used with some nouns, verbs, and adjectives.

miscounted	misjudged	misplaced	misspelled	misunderstood	misused

Complete each sentence with a word from the list. Check a dictionary if you don't know the meaning of a word.

The prefix *mis–* is spelled with only one *s*. But words like *misspell* that begin with *s* are spelled with a double *s*.

1. Matt made plans to see George after class, but he _____ where they were to meet. George went to the student center, but Matt went to the library.

2. Our teacher thought he had enough copies for everyone in class, but he _____. There are 14 students, and he had only 12 copies.

3. Abra really _____ her free time before class. She should have practiced her speech, but instead she checked her phone messages.

4. Chris wrote *recommend* with *cc*. If he had checked his dictionary, he wouldn't have _____ the word.

5. Teresa was late for work because she _____ her car keys and had to take the bus.

6. At first, Phillip didn't make eye contact when he spoke to people at work. As a result, some of his coworkers _____ him and thought he was unfriendly.

5. Suffixes *–er* and *–or*

The suffixes *–er* and *–or* mean "a person who." You can add *–er* and *–or* to some verbs to make nouns. For example, the verb *read + er = reader*, "a person who reads" and the verb *collect + or = collector*, "a person who collects."

The suffixes *–er* and *–or* can also mean "a thing that."

Complete the definitions on the right. Use the words on the left.

1. communicator   a. An _____ is a person or company that pays other people to work.

2. consumer   b. A _____ is a person who goes to see another person or place.

3. educator   c. A _____ is a person who translates from one language to another.

4. employer   d. A _____ is a person who buys or uses something.

5. translator   e. A _____ is a person who shares information, feelings, or ideas.

6. visitor   f. An _____ is a person who teaches.

6. Compound Words

Sometimes a compound word is written as one word. Sometimes there is space between words.

Complete the sentences. Use words from the list.

feedback	people skills	public speaking	teamwork

1. Everyone at work likes Hailey. She gets along with her coworkers and customers. She's got wonderful _____.

2. The _____ you get from your audience will be useful and will tell you how effective your presentation was.

3. _____ can help solve problems at work because it combines the skills and knowledge of a group of coworkers.

4. Shane doesn't like _____. He gets nervous when he has to talk in front of a large group.

7. Context Clues: General Clues

You can look for context clues, or hints that help you figure out an unknown word. An unfamiliar word may be related to the cause or effect of an action.

Read each sentence. Look for clues to help you understand the meaning of the boldfaced word. Write the meaning of the word on the line.

1. Negative body language such as crossing your arms is a **barrier** to effective communication. It stops information from getting across.

   A **barrier** is _____

2. Your **posture**, or the general way you hold your body, tells other people whether you are confident or not.

   Posture means _____

3. Feeling hungry, tired, or uncomfortable can **distract** you when you are trying to listen. These feelings take your attention away from what you are doing.

   To **distract** means _____

4. It's key to know your **audience** when you speak. Choose what you say and how you say it to fit the people who are watching or listening.

   An **audience** is _____

5. To communicate well, learn to see the world from another person's **perspective**, or point of view.

   Someone's **perspective** is _____

What is one way you could improve your verbal communication skills?

_____

8. Parts of Speech and the Dictionary

Some words can be used for more than one part of speech. For example, as a noun, *research* can mean "the study of something to learn more about it." (*He spoke to the class about his research.*) As a verb, *research* can mean "to look for information about." (*I need to go to the job center to research companies in the area.*)

Look up each boldfaced word in a dictionary. Write the definition that matches how the word is used in the sentence.

1. Effective speakers practice and **time** their presentations.

_____

2. When they speak, they **state** the message clearly and with confidence.

_____

3. They show **respect** for members of the audience and their perspectives.

_____

4. They **look** people directly in the eye. This makes them come across as friendly and confident.

_____

> In most dictionaries, words that are spelled the same but can be used as different parts of speech have separate word entries. The part of speech is part of the entry.

9. Multiple-Meaning Words

Some words have more than one meaning. To figure out a word's meaning, look at how it is used in the sentence. You can also look at nearby words for clues.

Look at the underlined word. Circle the letter of the best definition.

1. Ramona was very <u>open</u> when she spoke at the company meeting. She reacted thoughtfully to every question.
   a. to make ready for use
   b. willing to listen to other people

2. At graduation, the director of our program gave a <u>speech</u> about setting and meeting goals.
   a. a formal talk
   b. the ability to speak

3. Will's boss told him that if he wanted to get a promotion, it was <u>critical</u> for him to improve his communication skills.
   a. very important
   b. very serious or dangerous

4. Have you ever noticed how successful speakers <u>treat</u> their audiences?
   a. to handle or behave toward in a certain way
   b. to give medical attention to

5. The most important <u>tip</u> I read about improving my communication skills was about listening.
   a. extra money you give someone who has done work for you
   b. a small piece of advice

Unit 2 Review

Complete the paragraph. Use words from the list.

| effective | improve | key | perspectives | react | research | skills |

Next week Maya is going to present (1) _____ that she has done about safety in the warehouse. She asked her manager, Richard, for advice. "How can I (2) _____ the way I present myself to the team?"

Richard said he thought that it was (3) _____ for Maya to work on her speaking (4) _____. He suggested that she watch (5) _____ speakers online, on TV, and at work, and pay attention to what they do and how they (6) _____ to their audiences. He also told her to encourage her team members to share their opinions and (7) _____.

Complete Maya's notes from her conversation with Richard. Use words from the list.

| appreciate | confident | communication | cooperate | feedback | listener | message |

Ideas for Better (8) _____

☑ Remember to say "Thank you." Let the team know I
(9) _____ their presence at the meeting.

☑ Be (10) _____ . My coworkers will support
me if I speak up and make my points clearly.

☑ Share new and interesting information. Keep everyone
engaged and my (11) _____ clear.

☑ Ask questions and be a good (12) _____.
My team wants to (13) _____ with me,
and I'll learn from their (14) _____.

Read each question. Then circle the correct answer.

1. **Which definition of *key* matches the meaning in this sentence?**

   Knowing when to speak and what to say is <u>key</u> to success in the workplace.

   A the answers to questions in a textbook

   B something that opens a locked door

   C to put information into a computer using a keyboard

   D important and necessary

2. **What does the word *research* mean in this passage?**

   Eric took several months to decide what school he wanted to go to. He did a lot of <u>research</u> about schools with good communications departments.

   A to study something carefully

   B to collect information about a subject

   C careful study that is done to find information about something

   D to collect information for

3. **Which of these words means "spoken wrongly"?**

   A misspoken

   B unspoken

   C mispoken

   D spoke

4. **Which word or words from the passage mean about the same as *appreciated*?**

   Pam <u>appreciated</u> being asked to lead the class discussion. She knew it would be difficult for her to do, but she also recognized that taking the lead would help her confidence. She was grateful for the opportunity.

   A recognized

   B increased the value

   C was aware that

   D was grateful for

5. **What word best completes the passage?**

   Coco wants to work in the entertainment industry. She has many interests and a lot of _____ that will help her succeed.

   A skills

   B messages

   C barriers

   D time

6. **Which definition of *programmer* best matches the meaning in this sentence?**

   Julian is a software <u>programmer</u>. He writes code (instructions) for a large communications company in Portland.

   A a person who creates computer programs

   B a person who prepares entertainment program schedules

   C an electronic device that controls the operation of something

   D a person who prepares instructional programs

7. **What word best completes this sentence?**

   An effective work group needs openness, truth, and honest _____ to complete a job.

   A public speaking

   B teamwork

   C feedback

   D eye contact

8. **Which of these words is the opposite of *misheard*?**

   A heard incorrectly

   B heard correctly

   C understood wrongly

   D misunderstood

What can you do to improve your personal communication skills? Write your answer on a separate sheet of paper. Use at least six words you learned in this unit. Circle the vocabulary words you use.

Check your answers on page 104.

3 Finding a Place to Live

VOCABULARY

Read these words from the passage. Check the words you know.

- ☐ affordable
- ☐ apartment
- ☐ damage
- ☐ deposit
- ☐ lease
- ☐ location
- ☐ mortgage
- ☐ neighborhood
- ☐ owner
- ☐ repair
- ☐ roommate
- ☐ utilities

Where do you live? Do you live with a family member, rent a home, or own the home you live in? Why did you choose to live there?

It might be **affordable** to live with family members. But what if you want to rent your own place or even buy a home?

Renting an Apartment

Are you looking for an **apartment**? Think about how much you will be able to pay each month. Then list the things you need in an apartment.

- How many bedrooms and bathrooms do you need?

- Will you have a **roommate**? If you share an apartment, you can share the rent and other costs like **utilities**.

- Will you live close to work or school? Is the **neighborhood** safe?

How do you find an apartment? You can check the classified ads in the newspaper. You can also look online. Ads usually tell the size, **location**, and cost of rent. You will need to sign a **lease** that tells how many months you will rent the apartment. You must also pay a **deposit**. The **owner** can keep the deposit if you move out early or **damage** the apartment.

Buying a Home

Some people dream of owning a home. But there are many things to think about before you become a homeowner. Can you afford the costs of a home? Most buyers need a **mortgage**. People repay these home loans over many years.

Homeowners have costs that people who rent apartments don't have. They will need to pay taxes on the home. They will need to take care of the house and yard. And if something breaks, homeowners have to pay to **repair** it. They can't call a building manager for help.

Can you think of other words about renting or buying a home? Write them here.

_____ _____ _____

1. Vocabulary Focus

Write the word next to its definition.

affordable	apartment	damage	deposit
lease	location	mortgage	neighborhood
owner	repair	roommate	utilities

_____ 1. a place or position

_____ 2. a person who has or owns something

_____ 3. services offered to the public, such as electricity and water

_____ 4. a person that you share a room or home with

_____ 5. cheap enough that you can pay for something

_____ 6. to harm something

_____ 7. the act or result of fixing something

_____ 8. an area of a town or city

_____ 9. a set of rooms that you rent to live in

_____ 10. money paid before you rent something to make sure you don't damage it

_____ 11. an agreement that you will pay to live somewhere for a certain amount of time

_____ 12. a loan you get from a bank in order to pay for a home

2. Use the Vocabulary

Write about the kind of home you would like to live in. Use at least three words from the vocabulary list. Underline the vocabulary words you use.

_____

_____

_____

_____

_____

3. Work With New Vocabulary

Write your answers to the questions. Then compare answers with a partner.

1. Would you rather be an **owner** or a renter? Why?

   _____

2. What makes a person a good **roommate**?

   _____

3. What rooms can you usually find in an **apartment**?

   _____

4. Describe the **neighborhood** where you live.

   _____

The letter *t* in *mortgage* is silent.

5. Why does someone get a **mortgage**?

   _____

6. What are some **utilities** that you need in a home?

   _____

7. Name three things that might need a **repair**.

   _____

8. Why is the **location** of a home important?

   _____

9. Why is it important to read a **lease** carefully?

   _____

10. Is it fair for owners to charge a **deposit** when you rent an apartment? Why or why not?

    _____

11. What are some ways renters might **damage** an apartment?

    _____

12. Is the place where you live **affordable**? Explain why or why not.

    _____

4. Prefix re-

The prefix *re-* means "again" or "back." When this prefix is attached to a base word, you can usually figure out the word's meaning. For example, *replay* means "to play again." Sometimes *re-* is added to a root, as in *remember, response,* and *repair.* The meanings of these words are not as easy to figure out by breaking the words into parts.

Use words from the list to complete the sentences. Check a dictionary if you don't know the meaning of a word.

The prefix *re-* is common in English. But some words that start with *re* do **not** have a prefix. For example, in the words *real, reach,* and *read, re* does not mean "back" or "again." What other words do you know that do use *re-* as a prefix? Write them here.

rebuild	repaint	repay	replace	review

1. Lana got a mortgage to buy a house. She will _____ the money over 30 years.

2. Pat's young son drew on the walls of their apartment. Now Pat has to _____ the wall to cover the marks.

3. You should _____ a lease carefully before you sign it. Check that the important details are correct.

4. The stove in our apartment broke. The owner had to _____ it with a new stove.

5. The fire burned the apartment building, but the owners plan to _____ it next year.

_____

_____

_____

5. Suffix -able

The suffix *-able* means "can be done" or "able to be done." When this suffix is added to the end of a verb, the new word formed is an adjective. For example, the verb *enjoy + able = enjoyable,* an adjective that means that something can be enjoyed.

Use words from the list to complete the sentences. Check a dictionary if you don't know the meaning of a word.

affordable	available	comfortable	dependable	noticeable

1. Someone lives in the apartment now, but it will be _____ on October 1.

2. Eva is a _____ roommate. She always pays her part of the rent on time.

3. Apartments near my school cost a lot, but the ones near my job are _____.

4. The chairs in the living room are more _____ than the chairs in the kitchen.

5. The spots on the carpet were very _____, so Luis asked the owner to clean it.

6. Compound Words

You can often figure out the meaning of a compound word by looking at the two shorter words. For example, the word *homeowner* is made from the words *home* and *owner*. *Homeowner* means "a person who owns a home."

Complete the sentences. Use words from the list.

apartment building living room	bedroom newspaper	building manager roommates

1. Tony likes to sit on the sofa and watch TV in the _____.

2. We looked at the ads for apartments in the back of the _____.

3. Tara called the _____ and told him about the broken sink.

4. The _____ on Oak Street has 25 apartments.

5. Imani shares her apartment with two _____.

6. I can't sleep unless my _____ is very dark.

7. Context Clues: Synonyms and Examples

Look for clues when you see a word you don't know. See if the writer has used a synonym, or a word that means almost the same as the unknown word. The writer might use a synonym in the same sentence or in a nearby sentence.

You can also look for examples that will help you understand a word. The underlined examples help you understand what *utilities* means in this sentence:

Pedro pays $200 each month for utilities, including <u>electricity</u>, <u>gas</u>, and <u>water</u>.

Read the paragraph. Look for synonyms and examples that help you understand the boldfaced words. Then answer the questions.

Mr. Tran was the owner of a rental house, but he did not like being a **landlord**. His last **tenants** did a lot of **damage**. For example, there were spots on the carpet and holes in the walls. Mr. Tran needed to find some new renters. Kathy, Mia, and Sofia wanted to rent the house. They could split **expenses** such as rent, utilities, and food. Kathy said she would **purchase** some **furniture**, including a sofa, table, and chairs. Her friends could buy anything else they needed for the house.

1. What is a synonym for **landlord**? _____

2. What is a synonym for **tenants**? _____

3. What are the examples of **damage**? _____

4. What are the examples of **expenses**? _____

5. What is a synonym for **purchase**? _____

6. What are the examples of **furniture**? _____

8. The Dictionary and Multiple-Meaning Words

A dictionary can show several meanings for a word. Sometime a word can be used for more than one part of speech, such as a noun, verb, or adjective. To find the correct meaning in a dictionary, first choose the correct part of speech. Then think about the context and the topic you are reading about. Look for the definition that makes sense for your context and topic.

It is important to figure out the part of speech first when you look up a word's meaning. A word with several meanings can have one or more long entries in a dictionary. Reading only the meanings for the correct part of speech can help you find the right definition quickly.

Look at the underlined word. Figure out the part of speech. Then circle the letter of the best definition.

1. If you <u>break</u> your lease, you may lose your deposit.
   a. verb: to separate into pieces
   b. verb: to not keep an agreement
   c. noun: a short rest from work or school
   d. noun: a gap or opening

2. Luke wants to buy the empty <u>property</u> on Main Street and build a house on it.
   a. noun: the things that are owned by someone
   b. noun: a quality or characteristic
   c. noun: a piece of land
   d. noun: a home or other building

3. Tasha can't climb stairs, so she wants an apartment on the first <u>floor</u>.
   a. noun: a level or story of a building
   b. noun: the part of a room you stand on
   c. noun: the bottom of a sea or forest
   d. verb: to push down the gas pedal of a car and go fast

4. The landlord asked us for $700 rent and a $700 <u>deposit</u> when we signed our lease.
   a. noun: money that is put into a bank account
   b. noun: money paid before you rent something
   c. verb: to put an item down somewhere
   d. verb: to put money in a bank

5. Nicole's <u>share</u> of the rent is $400.
   a. noun: a part given by a person
   b. noun: a part of a company
   c. verb: to divide into parts
   d. verb: to tell your ideas and feelings to others

Look up these words in a dictionary. Write definitions that match the parts of speech.

6. complex   adjective: _____

　　　　　　　 noun: _____

7. safe   adjective: _____

　　　　　 noun: _____

Unit 3 Review

Complete the paragraphs. Use words from the lists.

affordable	available	bedrooms	location	newspaper	roommate

Olga is a student who is looking for a place to live. She doesn't have a lot of money, so she wants to find an

(1) _____ apartment. She read this ad in the (2) _____.

APARTMENTS

I am looking for a (3) _____ for an apartment with two (4) _____ and two bathrooms. The apartment is in a great (5) _____ near school and the city bus. It will be (6) _____ on August 1. $300 per month. No pets or smokers. Call 555-555-1234.

Olga decided to call about the apartment right away!

apartment building	building manager	comfortable	repairs

Will and Joan are also looking for a place to rent. But they have different ideas. Joan wants to rent a house. She

thinks a house with a yard will be more (7) _____ than an apartment. Will wants to move

to a new (8) _____. A new apartment won't need any (9) _____. If

something breaks, they can call the (10) _____ to fix it.

expenses	furniture	mortgage	purchase	repay	research

Do you want to own a house someday? If you do, it is important to (11) _____ the

costs. Most people who (12) _____ a home can't pay the full price all at once. They get a

(13) _____, which is a kind of home loan. They (14) _____ this loan

over many years. There are many other (15) _____ when you buy a home. For example, you

will need to buy (16) _____. You will also need to pay taxes and pay to fix things that break.

Read each question. Then circle the correct answer.

1. **Which definition of *deposit* matches the meaning in this sentence?**

   The water company asked for a $75 deposit before it would turn on the water.

   A an amount of money put into a bank

   B a layer of dirt left behind by water

   C money that must be paid before the start of a service

   D to place an item on a surface

2. **What does the word *neighborhood* mean in this passage?**

   Ali likes the neighborhood where his parents live. There are lots of shops and stores, and it is very safe.

   A a building with many apartments

   B an area of a town or city

   C a room that you sleep in

   D a place that you can afford

3. **Which of these words means "to look at again"?**

   A viewer

   B viewable

   C interview

   D review

4. **What is the meaning of *noticeable* in this sentence?**

   Hanna spilled a drink, and now there is a noticeable spot on the carpet.

   A The spot can be seen.

   B The spot is hard to find.

   C The spot can be cleaned.

   D The spot is a dark color.

5. **What does the word *damaged* mean in this sentence?**

   The renters damaged the walls when they left.

   A fixed

   B harmed

   C cleaned

   D moved

6. **Read this sentence:**

   Each month we pay $500 for rent and about $200 more for utilities in our apartment.

   Which of these is an example of a utility?

   A a mortgage

   B a bedroom

   C electricity

   D property

7. **Which word from the passage means about the same as *tenant*?**

   Jill lives in an apartment building. The tenant who lives above her is noisy. He plays loud music in his apartment late at night. Jill asked the building manager for help. He said he would talk to the renter.

   A apartment building

   B apartment

   C building manager

   D renter

8. **Which of these tells the rules for renting an apartment, such as the price and the number of months you will live there?**

   A section

   B mortgage

   C newspaper

   D lease

On a separate sheet of paper, write about the place where you live now or a place where you used to live. Use at least six words you learned in this unit. Circle the vocabulary words you use.

Check your answers beginning on page 104.

4 Getting Around Town

VOCABULARY

Read these words from the passage. Check the words you know.

- [ ] commute
- [ ] distance
- [ ] fare
- [ ] insurance
- [ ] maintenance
- [ ] public
- [ ] route
- [ ] schedule
- [ ] toll
- [ ] traffic
- [ ] transportation
- [ ] urban

Abbreviations

DMV (Department of Motor Vehicles)

SUV (sport utility vehicle)

mpg (miles per gallon)

mph (miles per hour)

How do you get to the places you need to go, like school, work, or the grocery store?

Transportation is how you get from one place to another. What's the best way to get around town? People in **urban** areas usually have choices. They can use **public** transportation, such as buses, subways, or trains. People who live or work outside of cities, though, may need cars.

Public Transportation

Public transportation is easy to use. Someone else does the driving. You can read, text, or talk while you **commute** to work or school. You won't have to find or pay for parking, but you will have to pay a **fare**.

To use public transportation, you will need to know **routes** and **schedules**. You will need to find out where the stops are and how long the trip will take. Usually buses have the largest number of routes, but they stop often and may get stuck in **traffic**. Trains and subways can be faster because they make fewer stops. However, they may not run frequently or at night.

Cars

Some people think a car is the best way to get around. With a car, you decide when and where you will go. You don't need to know routes or schedules, but you may need a map.

To drive, you will need a driver's license. You will also need **insurance**. If you drive into a city, you may need to pay for parking and **tolls**. Other costs include gas, **maintenance**, and repairs for the car.

Other Choices

If you don't want to drive or use public transportation, you can walk or ride a bike. These are free or low-cost ways to get around. They are also good forms of exercise. Just be sure you understand the **distance**, so you know how long it will take you to get where you are going.

Do you know any other words about transportation? Write them here.

_____   _____   _____

1. Vocabulary Focus

Write the word next to its definition.

commute route	distance schedule	fare toll	insurance traffic	maintenance transportation	public urban

You can pronounce the word *route* two ways. It can rhyme with *boot*, or it can rhyme with *out*. Either way, the *e* is silent.

_____ 1. the act or process of moving people from one place to another

_____ 2. the money that you pay to travel on a bus, train, plane, or other vehicle

_____ 3. to travel regularly between your home and another place, such as your job or school

_____ 4. related to a city

_____ 5. the amount of space between two places, points, or things

_____ 6. the money that you pay to drive on a road or across a bridge

_____ 7. a contract that you buy from a company in which the company agrees to pay for loss or damage

_____ 8. available for everyone to use and usually provided by the government

_____ 9. a path or way that a bus, train, or other vehicle regularly travels

_____ 10. all the vehicles moving on a street or road

_____ 11. the act of taking care of something by checking and fixing it

_____ 12. a list that tells when events will happen

2. Use the Vocabulary

What do you think transportation will be like 20 years from now? Use at least three vocabulary words. Underline the vocabulary words you use.

_____

_____

_____

_____

3. Work With New Vocabulary

Write your answers. Then compare answers with a partner.

1. Name three kinds of **transportation** you have used. Explain which one is best.

   _____

2. Give three examples of things you can find in an **urban** area.

   _____

3. Why is it important for a bus to follow a **schedule**?

   _____

4. Why do car drivers need **insurance**?

   _____

5. Besides transportation, what are some other places or things that are **public**?

   _____

6. How do you think people feel when they are stuck in **traffic**?

   _____

7. Should students have to pay **fares** to ride buses? Why or why not?

   _____

8. Describe how you **commute** to work or school. How long does the trip take?

   _____

9. Describe the **route** you use to get to work or school. What do you see along the way?

   _____

10. What kinds of places charge drivers a **toll**?

    _____

11. What are some examples of **maintenance** you must do on a car?

    _____

12. Describe the **distance** between your home and the places you go most often.

    _____

4. Root *trans*

The root *trans* means "across," "beyond," or "through." Read the definitions of these words with the root *trans*:

transport: to carry something from one place to another
transfer: to move from one place to another
transit: a system of trains and buses for moving people
translate: to change from one language to another
transparent: clear or see-through

Use words with the root trans *to complete the sentences.*

1. Fred needs to _____ from one bus to another at the downtown station.

2. Maria asked her friend to _____ the information into Spanish.

3. The city has a good _____ system with buses, trains, and a subway.

4. Jon keeps his bus pass in a _____ plastic sheet so that it's easy to see.

5. Buses will _____ people and their bags from the airport to the hotel.

> A **root** is a word part that can be combined with other roots, prefixes, or suffixes to form a word. Many English words have roots that come from Latin and Greek. You can use what you know about roots to figure out a word's meaning.

5. Suffix *–ly*

The suffix *–ly* means "characteristic of" or "in a way that is." When *–ly* is added to an adjective, the new word formed is an adverb. For example, the adjective *loud* + the suffix *–ly* = the adverb *loudly*, which means "in a way that is loud."

Use words from the list to complete the sentences. Check a dictionary if you don't know the meaning of a word.

easily	exactly	frequently	locally	quickly	usually

1. Karen walks to the farmer's market so she can shop for _____ grown food.

2. Bus fare is _____ $1.75. It doesn't matter when you travel; the cost is always the same.

3. Roberto _____ buys a weekly transit pass to save money.

4. Trains arrive _____ at that station, so if you miss one, another one will come soon.

5. If traffic is bad, Dana's commute can _____ take an hour or longer.

6. We walked _____ to the train station so that we wouldn't miss our train.

> When the suffix *–ly* is added to a noun, the new word formed is an adjective.
> friend/friendly
> man/manly
> mother/motherly
> month/monthly

6. Compound Words

The word *bike* is a short form of the word *bicycle*. Other examples of shortened words are:

gym (gymnasium)

fridge (refrigerator)

gas (gasoline)

phone (telephone)

You can figure out the meanings of many compound words by thinking about the meanings of the smaller words.

Write the compound word that matches the clue.

bike lane	parking lot	sidewalk	speed limit	traffic light

1. _____ : a place to walk on the side of a street

2. _____ : a light that tells traffic when to stop or go

3. _____ : an area in which people park cars

4. _____ : a lane or area of a street for bicycles

5. _____ : the limit for how fast you can drive

Complete each sentence with a compound word. Use a dictionary to check the meaning if you need to.

The meanings of some compound words are hard to figure out by looking at the individual words, for example, *landlord* or *butterfly*. You will need to look them up in a dictionary.

bus stop	crosswalk	highway	taxi driver	underground

6. Don drives on the _____ because it is faster than driving on city streets.

7. We saw the bus coming, so we ran to the _____.

8. The subway runs _____ through a system of tunnels.

9. The _____ is the safest place to cross a street.

10. The _____ asked Alberto where he wanted to go.

7. Context Clues: Synonyms and Antonyms

To figure out unknown words, you can look for synonyms, words with similar meanings. You can also look for antonyms, words with opposite or contrasting meanings.

Read the sentences. Underline words or phrases that mean something similar to the boldfaced words.

1. There were not enough seats for all the **passengers**. Some riders had to stand.

2. Traffic backed up for miles because of the **accident**. Fortunately, no one was hurt in the crash.

3. Emily's office building has parking for only 20 **vehicles**. After the spaces are full, people must park their cars on the street.

Read the sentences. Underline words or phrases with opposite or contrasting meanings to the boldfaced words.

These words may signal that a writer is contrasting two things: *but, on the other hand, in contrast, instead of, however, unlike.*

4. My sister likes to stay home during the holidays, but I like to **travel**.

5. The train is nearly empty when it **departs**. However, it's full by the time it arrives downtown.

6. Unlike drivers, who were stuck in traffic, **pedestrians** got to the outdoor concert on time.

8. Parts of Speech and the Dictionary

To figure out the meaning of a word, look at how it is used in the sentence.

Look up each boldfaced word in a dictionary. Write the definition that matches how the word is used in the sentence.

1. My transportation **pass** lets me ride the bus, train, and subway.

   _____

2. Passengers can **board** the train ten minutes before it leaves the station.

   _____

3. You are not allowed to **pass** a school bus when children are getting on or off.

   _____

4. Do you know which subway **line** goes downtown?

   _____

5. Buses **run** from 5 a.m. until midnight in that city.

   _____

6. Trains leave the **station** every 10 minutes on weekdays.

   _____

9. Multiple-Meaning Words

Some words have more than one meaning. To figure out the right meaning, look at how a word is used in its sentence. You can also look at nearby words for clues.

Look at the underlined word. Circle the letter of the best definition.

1. We got lost, so we stopped to ask for <u>directions</u>.
   a. instructions for how to get somewhere
   b. the lines along which something moves or points

2. Carrie thinks walking to work is a good <u>form</u> of exercise.
   a. the shape of a person or thing
   b. a type or variety

3. Nina has a short <u>drive</u> to work.
   a. to operate a vehicle
   b. a trip in a vehicle

4. Changing the oil in a car is an example of <u>routine</u> maintenance.
   a. the normal order of steps you follow to do something
   b. done in a regular way

Unit 4 Review

Complete the paragraphs. Use words from the lists.

Getting Around

When you visit our city, leave your car behind! Why spend your vacation sitting in (1) _____ or looking for a (2) _____? We have a great (3) _____ system that can take you where you want to go.

Trains and Buses

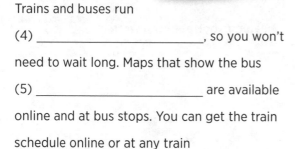

Trains and buses run (4) _____, so you won't need to wait long. Maps that show the bus (5) _____ are available online and at bus stops. You can get the train schedule online or at any train

(6) _____. If you plan to use public transportation often, think about buying a transit pass. A transit pass costs less than paying the (7) _____ each time you take a bus or train.

Walking and Biking

Do you like to walk or ride a bike? Walking and biking are great ways to see the city. Special paths for (8) _____ and bicycles lead into the downtown area. Once downtown, you can walk along wide (9) _____ as you check out the shops and restaurants.

Gina drove her car downtown one day. The (10) _____ in front of her changed from yellow to red. Gina (11) _____ hit her brakes. But the (12) _____ behind her did not stop in time. It hit the back of Gina's car. Gina had never been in an (13) _____ before. She and the other driver (14) _____ pulled their cars to the side of the street. Gina asked the other driver if he and his (15) _____ were OK. Then she looked at the damage to her car. She hoped the other driver had good (16) _____!

Read each question. Then circle the correct answer.

1. **Which definition of *line* matches the meaning in this sentence?**

   The car crossed the center <u>line</u> and almost caused an accident.

   A a row of words on a page

   B a row of people next to one another

   C a long thin mark on the ground

   D a transportation route

2. **What does the word *transatlantic* mean in this passage?**

   Some of the first <u>transatlantic</u> airplane flights took more than 30 hours. Today it takes only about 7 to 8 hours to fly between New York and London.

   A under the Atlantic Ocean

   B similar to the Atlantic Ocean

   C around the Atlantic Ocean

   D across the Atlantic Ocean

3. **What does the word *tolls* mean in this passage?**

   New roads are very expensive to build. That is why some places charge <u>tolls</u> on new roads. You can usually drive for free on an older road, but it will be slower than the new one.

   A money you pay to ride public transportation

   B money you pay to drive on a road or bridge

   C money you pay to get car insurance

   D money you pay to take care of a car

4. **Which of these compound words means "a place where people are able to walk across a street"?**

   A bus stop

   B parking lot

   C sidewalk

   D crosswalk

5. **Which word best completes the sentence?**

   Bill _____ about 25 miles each day between his home and work.

   A transports

   B commutes

   C departs

   D passes

6. **Read this sentence.**

   Our city has an excellent and affordable <u>public transportation</u> system.

   Which of these is a kind of public transportation?

   A a motorcycle

   B a bicycle

   C a car

   D a subway

7. **Which word from the passage means about the same as *depart*?**

   Larry needs to go downtown this morning. He checks the train schedule online. A train <u>departs</u> at 7:05 a.m. If Larry misses that train, the next one leaves at 7:45. Larry hurries to get ready.

   A checks

   B misses

   C leaves

   D hurries

8. **Which word best completes the sentence?**

   With my bus _____, I can ride the bus as much as I want for a month.

   A pass

   B station

   C lane

   D stop

Describe the ways people in your community get around. Write your answer on a separate sheet of paper. Use at least six words you learned in this unit. Circle the vocabulary words you use.

Check your answers on page 105.

5 Finding a Job

VOCABULARY

Read these words from the passage. Check the words you know.

- ☐ apply
- ☐ career
- ☐ control
- ☐ decrease
- ☐ details
- ☐ employment
- ☐ leads
- ☐ networking
- ☐ organize
- ☐ routine
- ☐ search
- ☐ training

Finding a job is one of the most important things you'll ever have to do in life. A job search can take weeks or months, so it's key to have a plan in place before you start.

Take Charge

You need to be the boss of your job **search**. Planning and keeping everything you need in one place makes it easier to focus on your goal—getting the perfect job. So, **organize** all of your important information. Include **details** about your education as well as your skills and any work experience or **training** you have.

Set Goals

Looking for **employment** is hard work, but you can make it easier if you set small goals that you can **control**. For example, you can't control when you'll get a job, but you can control how many jobs you **apply** for. If you keep your goals manageable, you'll have a lot of little successes along the way.

Manage Your Time

Finding a job is your job, so you need to create a regular **routine**, just as you would at a real job. Set a specific time to start and end your job search each day. Take breaks as you would at work. But don't think about your job search all the time. Make time to do something not related to looking for a job. Go for a walk (exercise is a great way to **decrease** stress), spend time with your family, or start a hobby. Otherwise you may find it difficult to balance your job search with the rest of your life.

Find a Support System

Looking for a job can wear you out, especially if you've been looking for a long time, so it's important to have a positive attitude. It helps to interact with other job hunters and with professional **career** counselors. They can provide support and be great resources. They may give you search tips or recommend job **leads**. Look for support at online **networking** sites, the library, or a local job center.

Do you know any other words about looking for a job? Write them here.

_____   _____   _____

1. Vocabulary Focus

Write the word next to its definition.

apply	career	control	decrease	detail	employment
lead	networking	organize	routine	search	training

_____ 1. a small item; a particular thing

_____ 2. a regular course of action

_____ 3. a tip or clue

_____ 4. a job that you learn to do and then do for many years

_____ 5. to put or arrange things in order

_____ 6. understanding or skills gained from practice or activity

_____ 7. interacting with other people to exchange information and make contacts

_____ 8. to manage

_____ 9. the condition of having a job

_____ 10. when you try to find something

_____ 11. to ask for employment

_____ 12. to become less or smaller

2. Use the Vocabulary

Choose three of the vocabulary words. Define them in your own words.

1. _____

2. _____

3. _____

Share your definitions with a partner. Talk about them, and make suggestions for revising them. Rewrite your definitions and show them to your teacher.

3. Work With New Vocabulary

Write your answers. Then compare answers with a partner.

1. What **career** you are interested in? What career would you never be interested in?

    _____

2. Name three jobs that require special **training**.

    _____

3. Would you rather **apply** for a job in person or online? Why?

    _____

4. How do you **decrease** the stress in your life?

    _____

5. You can get a **lead** on a job opening. What are two other things you can get a lead on?

    _____

6. What's your daily **routine**?

    _____

7. What are three things you **control**?

    _____

8. Why is it helpful to **organize** a job hunt?

    _____

9. What is the hardest thing about finding **employment**?

    _____

10. How long do you think a job **search** usually takes?

    _____

11. Write a **detail** related to your education or training.

    _____

12. Why is **networking** helpful when you're looking for a job?

    _____

4. Prefix *inter-*

When *inter-* is at the beginning of a word, it can mean "between" or "among." When the prefix is attached to a base word, you can usually figure out the word's meaning. For example, *interstate* means "between states." Sometimes *inter-* is added to a word root, as in *interfere*.

Match the word with its definition. Write the correct letter.

_____ 1. interact

_____ 2. Internet

_____ 3. interpersonal

_____ 4. interrupt

_____ 5. interview

a. to stop something from being completed

b. related to relationships and communication

c. a meeting between a person applying for a job and the person offering the job

d. to communicate or share with

e. the worldwide computer network

> Some words begin with *inter-*, but do not use those letters as a prefix. For example, your *interests* are your favorite activities.

5. Suffix *-ing*

When the suffix *-ing* is added to a verb, that verb can become a noun. The noun is the action of, process of, result of, or something connected with the verb. For example, if you add *-ing* to the verb *network*, you get the action *networking*.

Rewrite the words below. Add -ing.

1. apply _____

2. look _____

3. make _____

4. stop _____

5. take _____

6. train _____

Check your answers above. Then use the words to complete the sentences below. Check a dictionary if you don't know the meaning of a word.

7. _____ a few short breaks during the day makes my job search feel less stressful.

8. Hannah starts every day by _____ a list of her goals.

9. Eli got his job by _____ for one he found online.

10. The career counselor suggested _____ our job hunt at 5:00 every day, just as if we were working at a regular job.

11. What kind of _____ do you need to be a medical technician?

12. Monica goes to job interviews _____ her best.

> For one syllable verbs that have a middle short vowel and end with a single consonant, double the final consonant and add *-ing*. (example: *nap, napping*)
>
> For verbs that end in silent *e*, drop the *e* and add *-ing*. (example: *date, dating*)

6. Compound Words

Sometimes a compound word is written as one word, sometimes there is a space between words, and sometimes there is a – (hyphen) between words.

Write the compound word that matches the clue.

full-time	job application	workshop

1. _____ : a form you complete with information about your life, skills, experience, etc. when you are looking for work

2. _____ : a class in which a small group of people learns the skills to do something

3. _____ : for all the normal working hours of the day or week

Complete each sentence with a compound word. Use a dictionary to check the meaning if you need to.

background	job fair	paperwork

4. Gene had to complete a lot of _____ to apply for a job with the government. There were many forms to complete.

5. On Saturday, there's a _____ at the school where job hunters can meet with local employers.

6. The job application asked for my educational _____, my experience, training, and education.

7. Context Clues: Definitions

If you don't know the meaning of a word, look for context clues. A context clue may be the definition of the word.

Read the sentences. Look for clues to help you understand the meanings of the boldfaced words. Write the meaning of each word on the line.

1. Jack is applying for an **apprenticeship** at the job center. He'll get job training and classroom instruction at the same time.

   An *apprenticeship* is _____

2. A job fair is a great **opportunity**, or chance, to interview for several positions during a single day.

   An *opportunity* is _____

3. What career are you interested in? Make a list of the abilities or experience the career requires. Do you have any of those **qualifications**?

   Qualifications are _____

4. If you need help choosing a career, you might want to take a career **assessment**. The test helps identify your skills and the jobs that match them.

   An *assessment* is _____

8. Parts of Speech and the Dictionary

To figure out the meaning of a word, look at how it is used in the sentence.

Look at each boldfaced word. What part of speech does it play? Circle noun or verb. Then look up the word in a dictionary. Write the correct definition on the line.

noun   verb   1. **Monitor** the websites of companies you want to work for. Check their job listings at least once a week.

_____

noun   verb   2. The director of the career center says she's going to **post** new jobs on Monday morning.

_____

noun   verb   3. Build a **network** of friends, ex-employers, and coworkers who can help you with your job search.

_____

noun   verb   4. Sharyn is going to **train** to be a web developer.

_____

9. Multiple-Meaning Words

Some words have more than one meaning. To figure out the right meaning, look at how a word is used in the sentence. You can also look at nearby words for clues.

Look at the underlined word. Circle the letter of the best definition.

1. Kent got a great job <u>lead</u> from a friend who works at the library.
   a. the first place
   b. information that may be helpful

2. The new tech-support center is going to <u>employ</u> about 75 new workers.
   a. to give work to
   b. to make use of

3. As part of her job search, Emily Ann is making professional <u>connections</u> at the job center.
   a. place where two things join
   b. relationships between people or groups

4. Join a job <u>club</u> and interact with other people.
   a. an organization of people with a common interest who meet regularly
   b. a heavy stick

5. <u>Contact</u> people by phone and follow up with an email or thank-you note.
   a. touch
   b. communicate with

Complete the paragraphs. Use words from the lists.

apply	leads	networking	organize	search	training

Some Dos and Don'ts for Job Hunters

▶ Don't (1) _____ for every job you find. Focus only on jobs you're interested in and have the qualifications for.

▶ Do get as much (2) _____ as you can. Find out what kinds of free courses are available at your local job or workforce development center. The more skills you have, the better your chance of getting the job you want.

▶ Do follow up on all job (3) _____. People want to help you, but it's up to you to do the work and make the connection.

▶ Don't think about your job (4) _____ all the time. Make time for the other things and people that you care about.

▶ Do try to (5) _____ as much of your job search as you can. Make lists of jobs you've applied for. Make lists of your skills and education. Make lists of helpful (6) _____ sites. Make lots of lists!

Help Send feedback Privacy Terms

career	control	decrease	details	employment	routine

When Eddie lost his job at the club, he decided it was time for a change. To help him make a smart decision about a new (7) _____, Eddie spoke to a counselor at the city workforce department. They talked about what Eddie wanted from a job.

Eddie realized that the most important thing for him was to (8) _____ his time better. He realized that he wanted a full-time job with a regular (9) _____. He thought that working from 9:00 to 5:00, Monday to Friday, would (10) _____ the stress in his life and allow him to spend more time with his family.

The counselor suggested that Eddie take an (11) _____ assessment to find out what kind of work would fit him best. She also asked Eddie a lot of questions, including the (12) _____ of his education, training, and other life experience.

Read each question. Then circle the correct answer.

1. **What does the word *international* mean in this passage?**

   Trevor's Dog Treats have become so successful that the company has gone international, opening stores all around the world.

   A among nations

   B without any nations

   C above nations

   D against nations

2. **Which word from the passage means about the same as *opportunity*?**

   When you're at an event like a job fair, take advantage of every opportunity you get to talk to people. Each time you have a chance to make a connection, you're growing your network.

   A event

   B chance

   C connection

   D network

3. **Which of these compound words means "someone's previous education, experience, and training"?**

   A part-time

   B paperwork

   C background

   D job fair

4. **Which word best completes the sentence?**

   If Deshawn goes to the new vocational school in Lockhart, he can do an _____ in the tech program.

   A club

   B opportunity

   C apprenticeship

   D routine

5. **Which word best completes the sentence?**

   Anne is going to _____ at next week's job fair. She won't make any money, but she may meet her future employer.

   A lead

   B volunteer

   C apply

   D contact

6. **Which of these is a way to *organize* your job search?**

   A See a career counselor.

   B Take a break.

   C Make a list.

   D Interact with other job hunters.

7. **Which definition of *training* matches the meaning in this sentence?**

   Nekia is training to become a photographer.

   A learning a skill through practice

   B pointing something, like a camera, at

   C preparing physically

   D directing the growth of a plant

8. **What does the word *apply* mean in this passage?**

   Derrick decided to apply only for jobs he found online. He thought that the Internet was the best place to find work.

   A to have a connection

   B to bring into action

   C to make a written request

   D to put onto

Imagine your next job search. On a separate sheet of paper, write about what you will do to get the best possible job. Use at least six words you learned in this unit. Circle the vocabulary words you use.

Check your answers on page 105.

6 Banking

VOCABULARY

Read these words from the passage. Check the words you know.

- [ ] account
- [ ] automatically
- [ ] balance
- [ ] debit card
- [ ] deposit
- [ ] electronically
- [ ] fee
- [ ] interest
- [ ] manage
- [ ] minimum
- [ ] service
- [ ] withdraw

Abbreviations

ATM (Automated Teller Machine)

NSF (non-sufficient funds)

What kinds of bank accounts do you have? How is using a bank helpful?

Types of Accounts and Services

Banks offer safe places to save and **manage** your money. Most banks offer several types of **accounts**. In a savings account, you can save for future expenses. Many savings accounts pay **interest**, which helps your money grow.

Banks also offer checking accounts. You **deposit** money that you use for paying bills. There are several ways to **withdraw** the money. You can write checks or use a **debit card** in stores. You can get cash from an ATM or from a teller inside your bank.

Most banks offer other **services**, too. For example, you can get money orders, loans, and safe-deposit boxes for storing valuable items.

Choosing an Account

Banks often charge **fees**, so it's important to choose the right bank and the right account. Here are a few things to think about:

- Is there a **minimum** amount you must deposit to open an account?
- Does the bank charge a monthly fee for an account?
- How much does the bank charge if you bounce a check?
- Will you earn interest on your **balance**?
- Does the bank charge you for writing checks or using an ATM?

Online Banking

Today you can do a lot of banking online. In fact, some banks don't even have branches. With online banking, you can view your account balance and statements and keep track of your money. Many banks offer an online bill pay service, too. To pay bills online, you enter your payment information, and the bank pays the bill **electronically**. You don't need to worry about writing and mailing a check.

With direct deposit, you don't need to take your paycheck to the bank. It is deposited into your bank account **automatically**. Your money is available right away.

Do you know any other words about banks? Write them here.

_____ _____ _____

1. Vocabulary Focus

Write the word next to its definition.

account	automatically	balance	debit card
deposit	electronically	fee	interest
manage	minimum	service	withdraw

In the word *debit* the letter *e* has a short *e* sound. But in the word *deposit* the letter *e* has a short *i* sound.

_____ 1. the extra money that you earn when you save money, or the extra money you pay when you borrow money

_____ 2. the amount of money in a bank account

_____ 3. an arrangement in which a bank keeps records of the money a person puts in and takes out of the bank

_____ 4. work that a business does and offers to its customers

_____ 5. a way of sending information by a piece of equipment such as a computer

_____ 6. the smallest amount or lowest that is allowed or needed

_____ 7. to take money out of a bank account

_____ 8. done in such a way that a person does not need to act or think

_____ 9. to put money into a bank account

_____ 10. an amount of money that you pay for a service

_____ 11. a plastic card that you use to take money from a bank account instead of writing a check

_____ 12. to make decisions about and take control of something

2. Use the Vocabulary

How is banking online different from going into a bank in person? Use at least three vocabulary words. Underline the vocabulary words you use.

_____

_____

_____

_____

_____

3. Work With New Vocabulary

Write your answers. Then, compare answers with a partner.

1. Name at least two ways you can **withdraw** money from a bank account.

   _____

2. Why do people like to have their pay go into the bank **automatically**?

   _____

3. How do you **manage** your money?

   _____

4. What bank **services** do you use now or will you use in the future?

   _____

5. Besides banks, what other places or services charge people **fees**?

   _____

6. Would you rather have a large or small **balance** in your bank account? Explain why.

   _____

7. Why do people **deposit** their money in banks?

   _____

8. Describe how using a **debit card** is different from writing a check.

   _____

9. Would you rather pay **interest** on a loan or earn **interest** on a savings account? Why?

   _____

10. What are three things you can do **electronically**?

   _____

11. In your own words, describe what a bank **account** is.

   _____

12. What is the **minimum** age to drive and to vote? Can you think of anything else that has a minimum number to do something?

   _____

4. Prefix *over-*

The prefix *over-* means "too much" or "above." Usually the prefix *over-* is added to a verb. For example, when you *overeat*, you eat too much.

Read each word and its definition. Then use the word in a sentence.

1. overpaid: paid too much

_____

2. overworked: made to work too hard

_____

3. overreact: to react or respond too strongly and with too much emotion

_____

4. overdraft: the money you owe a bank when you have spent more money than you have in your account

_____

5 overtime: time spent at work beyond normal working hours

_____

6. overspend: to spend too much

_____

5. Suffix *–al*

The suffix *–al* means "related to" or "associated with." The suffix *–al* can be added to a noun to make an adjective, such as *nature* → *natural*. It can also be added to a verb to make a noun, such as *arrive* → *arrival*.

Use words from the list to complete the sentences. Check a dictionary if you don't know the meaning of a word.

> When a word ends in *e*, drop the *e* before adding the suffix *–al*. For example, *refuse* becomes *refusal*.

approval	central	educational	financial	withdrawal

1. A _____ planner can help you plan how to manage and save money.

2. The main reason we opened an account at that bank was because of its

   _____ location.

3. Gloria got _____ for a new car loan.

4. Jacob made a _____ from his savings account to pay for his classes.

5. My bank offers _____ programs to teach people about credit.

6. Compound Words

Look at each part of a compound word to figure out its meaning.

Match each compound word with the correct definition.

_____ 1. checkbook

a. a document similar to a check that you buy to pay someone

_____ 2. deposit slip

b. the day that you get paid

_____ 3. direct deposit

c. a small book of checks that you get from your bank

_____ 4. money order

d. a way of getting your pay put directly into your bank account

_____ 5. paycheck

e. a person whose job is to guard a bank and keep it safe and secure

_____ 6. payday

f. a check you get for the money you earned from a job

_____ 7. security guard

g. a piece or slip of paper that you fill out to make a deposit

7. Context Clues: General Clues

Look for clues in the same and nearby sentences to figure out the meanings of unknown words. For example, you can think about whether a word names a person, thing, or idea (a noun), or whether it tells an action (a verb).

Read the sentences. Look for clues that help you understand the meanings of underlined words. Circle the letter of the correct meaning.

1. I handed my check to the <u>teller</u>. She asked if I wanted to deposit it into my checking or my savings account.
   a. a person who works in a bank
   b. a person who tells stories at work

2. The teller looked at the back of my check. She said, "I can't deposit this yet. You will need to <u>endorse</u> it." Then she handed me a pen.
   a. to tear into small pieces
   b. to sign the back of a check before you deposit it

3. Yoko wants to buy a car, but she doesn't have enough money. She is going to ask the bank for a <u>loan</u>.
   a. an amount of money that you get from a bank and pay back over time
   b. a car that you can borrow but don't own

4. The banker asked Yoko to bring some <u>documents</u> with her, such as her driver's license and a copy of her most recent paycheck.
   a. papers that you write for school
   b. pieces of paper that have important information

8. Parts of Speech and the Dictionary

To figure out the meaning of a word, look at how it is used in the sentence.

Look up each boldfaced word in a dictionary. Write the part of speech and the definition that matches how the word is used in the sentence.

1. Dana asked the teller how long it would take for a check to **clear** her account.

   _____

2. The bank charged me a $25 fee by mistake. They agreed to **credit** my account.

   _____

3. The banker said that Rick had poor **credit**, so the bank would not give him a loan.

   _____

4. Luis does not have enough **funds** in his account to pay for the trip.

   _____

5. I went to the ATM to get **cash**.

   _____

6. Some businesses charge a fee to **cash** a paycheck, so I usually go to my bank.

   _____

> Before you look up a word in a dictionary, know what part of speech you are looking for.
>
> - If a word names a person, place, thing, or idea, it is a noun.
> - If a word tells an action, it is a verb.
> - If a word describes a noun, it is an adjective.

9. Multiple-Meaning Words

Words can have multiple meanings. Think about the topic you are reading about. The topic can provide important clues about the correct meaning.

Look at each underlined word. Circle the letter of the best definition.

1. Be careful not to <u>bounce</u> a check because the bank will charge you a fee.
   a. to make a ball or other object hit a surface and come back up in the air
   b. to have a check refused by the bank because there is not enough money in the account

2. The nearest <u>branch</u> of my bank is 20 miles away, so I do not go there often.
   a. a local part of a larger business
   b. a part of a tree that grows from the trunk

3. I used a <u>slip</u> of paper to add the amounts of the checks.
   a. a small mistake
   b. a small piece

4. Jack and Judy Stern got <u>approval</u> for a bank loan.
   a. a feeling that someone or something is good
   b. a decision to accept a plan

Unit 6 Review

Read about Tricia and how she managed her money. Complete each part with words from the list.

additional	overtime	overworked	paycheck

Tricia has a job in a factory. Last week, Tricia's boss asked her to work (1) _____. Tricia didn't want to be (2) _____. She had a busy life with work, school, and family. But she knew that her (3) _____ would be bigger if she worked more hours. And she really needed the (4) _____ money.

account	balance	bounced	fee	financial	overspent

The month before, Tricia had made some poor (5) _____ decisions. She had (6) _____ at the shopping mall, buying things that she didn't really need. Then her car had broken down. She wrote a check to pay for the repairs. But she didn't check her (7) _____ first. Tricia had $120 in her (8) _____, but she wrote a check for $300. As a result, the check (9) _____. Her bank charged her a $35 (10) _____ for not having enough money there.

automatically	deposit	deposit slip	direct deposit	payday	security guard	teller

So Tricia agreed to work extra hours at the factory. On (11) _____, Tricia picked up her check. She was pleased about the extra money she had earned. After work, she hurried to the bank to (12) _____ the check. She got there just before closing time. The (13) _____ was just about to lock the door. Tricia quickly filled out the (14) _____ and waited in line. When it was her turn, Tricia handed the check to the (15) _____.

"I was afraid the bank would be closed before I got here," she said.

"Have you thought about using (16) _____?" he asked. "You don't have to come in to the bank when you get paid. Your employer can put your money into your account (17) _____."

"No, but am I going to look into it," Tricia replied.

Read each question. Then circle the correct answer.

1. **Which definition of *credit* matches the meaning in this sentence?**

   The bank gave me a $50 <u>credit</u> for opening a new account.

   A approval for doing something well

   B a unit of study at a college or university

   C money that a bank lets you borrow or use

   D money given to you

2. **Which of these words means "paid too much"?**

   A overdraft

   B overpaid

   C payday

   D paycheck

3. **Which words from the passage mean about the same as *endorse*?**

   The teller asked Bella to <u>endorse</u> her check. Bella turned the check over. She signed her name. She wanted to deposit the check, so she also wrote her account number on the back.

   A turned the check over

   B signed her name

   C wanted to deposit

   D wrote her account number

4. **What does the word *withdraw* mean in this passage?**

   Tom can <u>withdraw</u> no more than $400 a day from the ATM. If he needs more cash, he must go inside the bank.

   A take out

   B put in

   C borrow

   D overspend

5. **Read this information about a bank account. What does the word *minimum* mean?**

   The <u>minimum</u> opening deposit for a savings account is $25.

   A the most you can add

   B the smallest amount needed

   C the amount you pay each month

   D the fee you pay for online banking

6. **Which meaning of *branches* matches how the word is used in this sentence?**

   We opened an account at G&W Bank because it has <u>branches</u> all over town, including one near our apartment.

   A local offices of a larger company

   B parts of government

   C groups of family members

   D parts of an area of study or learning

7. **Which of these compound words means "a small book of printed checks"?**

   A checking account

   B paycheck

   C checkbook

   D checkmark

8. **Which word best completes the passage?**

   At Best Bank, we offer many _____. For example, you can get loans, buy money orders, and use our online banking system.

   A customers

   B withdrawals

   C fees

   D services

How can banks help people manage their money? Write your answer on a separate sheet of paper. Use at least six words you learned in this unit. Circle the vocabulary words you use.

Check your answers starting on page 105.

7 Paying for Purchases

VOCABULARY

Read these words from the passage. Check the words you know.

- [ ] budget
- [ ] cashier
- [ ] checkout line
- [ ] convenient
- [ ] credit card
- [ ] identification
- [ ] insert
- [ ] payment
- [ ] purchases
- [ ] receipt
- [ ] scan
- [ ] self-checkout

Abbreviations

I.D. (identification)

PIN (personal identification number)

Do you enjoy shopping? Think about the things you buy every week. Think about the things you rarely buy. How do you usually pay for things?

For most people, the fun part of shopping is choosing **purchases**. Paying for them is not as much fun.

Waiting to Pay

At most stores, you have to stand in a **checkout line** to pay. Sometimes there are a lot of people in line, and you have to wait a long time. But finally, you reach the **cashier**. She usually enters or **scans** your purchases for you.

In some stores, you can scan your own purchases. That's called "**self-checkout**." There is no cashier. The computer screen tells you how much to pay.

Ways to Pay

There are lots of ways to pay for your purchases. Many people like to pay with cash. It's **convenient** to use because all stores take cash. And cash can help you **budget** your money. If you pay with cash, you know exactly how much money you have to spend.

Some businesses take checks as **payment**. Checks are printed with information about you, your bank, and your bank account. Sometimes you have to show **identification** (I.D.) to pay by check.

Debit cards and **credit cards** may be the most popular forms of payment. You **insert** your card into a card reader. You may have to enter your PIN (personal identification number) or sign your name. If you don't want to carry around a lot of cash, debit and credit cards are convenient and easy ways to pay.

Whether you pay with cash, by check, or with a debit or credit card, always ask for and save your **receipt**. You will need it if you want to return your purchases.

Do you know any other words about shopping? Write them here.

_____ _____ _____

1. Vocabulary Focus

Match the word with its definition. Write the correct letter.

_____ 1. budget

_____ 2. cashier

_____ 3. checkout line

_____ 4. convenient

_____ 5. credit card

_____ 6. identification

_____ 7. insert

_____ 8. payment

_____ 9. purchases

_____ 10. receipt

_____ 11. scan

_____ 12. self-checkout

a. the line in a store where you wait to pay for things you are buying

b. a plastic card that you use to buy something now and pay it for later

c. things that you have bought

d. to put something inside of something else

e. an amount of money you give when you buy something

f. a plan for spending money

g. a piece of paper that shows you have paid for something

h. to use a machine to read coded information

i. the person who takes money in a store

j. an area of a store with machines that shoppers use to pay for items without a cashier

k. easy and quick

l. a card or document that shows who you are

The *p* in *receipt* is silent.

2. Use the Vocabulary

Write about the last time you went shopping and made a purchase. Use at least three words from the vocabulary list. Underline the vocabulary words you use.

_____

_____

_____

_____

_____

3. Work With New Vocabulary

Answer the questions. Then compare answers with a partner.

1. What do you do with your **receipt** after you buy something?

   _____

2. What are the last three **purchases** you made?

   _____

3. Why do you think stores have **self-checkout**?

   _____

4. How carefully do you **budget** your money?

   _____

5. What is the longest time you've ever waited in a **checkout line**?

   _____

6. What skills does a **cashier** need?

   _____

7. Would you rather pay for a purchase with cash or with a **credit card**? Why?

   _____

8. What form of **identification** do you have with you right now? What information does it have about you?

   _____

9. Why do you have to **insert** a credit card or debit card into a machine?

   _____

10. What happens when you forget to make an important **payment** like your rent or a credit card bill?

    _____

11. Is the most **convenient** place to shop always the best place to shop? Why or why not?

    _____

12. Do the cashiers where you like to shop **scan** your purchases or do they enter the prices?

    _____

4. Prefix *pre-*

The prefix *pre-* means "before." The prefix *pre-* comes before a base word, for example, *preschool*. *Pre-* can also come before a word root that cannot stand alone without the prefix, as in *predict*.

The underlined word in each sentence starts with the prefix pre-. *Write the definition of the underlined word. Use a dictionary to check your answers.*

1. We can <u>preview</u> the sales items online.

   definition: _____

2. Credit card companies often <u>preapprove</u> customers for new credit cards.

   definition: _____

3. Users can <u>prepay</u> for minutes on some cell phone plans.

   definition: _____

4. You can <u>preorder</u> the newest book from your favorite writer on that website.

   definition: _____

5. The store will <u>presell</u> the new computers in August and ship them in December.

   definition: _____

> You know that you take a pretest before you take the real test. What other words do you know that use *pre-* as a prefix? Write them here.
>
> _____
>
> _____
>
> _____

5. Suffix *-ment*

The suffix *-ment* means the action or result of a verb. You can add *-ment* to some verbs to make nouns. For example, the verb *pay* + *ment* = *payment*, "the action of paying."

Complete each sentence. Use a word from the list.

advertisement	agreement	employment	payment	shipment	statement

1. We get a bank _____ showing our balance each month.

2. Before you can get a credit card, you have to sign the _____. It explains all the rules for using the card.

3. The new mall will provide _____ for hundreds of people.

4. This _____ from the newspaper shows everything that is on sale at Metro Market this week.

5. Eric and Sarah bought a car for $3,700 last year. They make a _____ of $250 on it every month.

6. The new smart phones sold out right away, but the salesperson said he would get another _____ tomorrow.

6. Compound Words

A compound word is made by putting two or three words together to make a new word. Sometimes a compound word is written as one word, for example, *salesperson*. Sometimes there is space between the words, as in *credit card*.

Complete each sentence. Use words from the list.

barcode downtown	checkbook online shopping	checkout line sales tax	clearance sale salesperson

1. There were eight people ahead of me in the _____. I didn't want to wait, so I used self-checkout.

2. Her new shoes cost $49, but with the _____, the total was $53.17.

3. We were really lucky. The store was having a _____, so we got the sofa for 25% off.

4. Don left his _____ at home, so he paid for his purchases with cash.

5. The _____ at the electronics store helped them choose the best TV.

6. I like to shop _____. My friends would rather shop at the mall.

7. The computer "reads" the _____ when the cashier scans your purchases.

8. Many people prefer _____ because they don't have to leave the house.

7. Context Clues: Definitions and Synonyms

If you don't know the meaning of a word, look for clues. Sometimes authors include a definition of a word. Authors may also use a synonym, or a word with a similar meaning, in the same or nearby sentences.

Read each sentence. Look for clues to help you understand the meaning of the boldfaced word. Write the meaning on the line.

1. Once a year, Mitchell's Department Store offers a **discount**, or a percent off the price, to its regular customers.

   A *discount* is _____

2. The shirt didn't fit, so Frank decided to **exchange** it. He returned it for a different size.

   To *exchange* means _____

3. I tried to **swipe** my debit card in the machine, but the cashier asked me to slide it again.

   To *swipe* means _____

4. The website will **ship** the computer tomorrow. They're charging me $18 to mail it.

   To *ship* means _____

5. The milk was sour, so Mimi asked the store for a **refund**. She wanted to get her money back.

   A *refund* is _____

8. Parts of Speech and the Dictionary

Some words can be used for more than one part of speech. For example, as a noun *shop* can mean "a store." As a verb, *shop* can mean "to buy things."

Look at each boldfaced word. What part of speech does it play? Circle noun *or* verb. *Then look up the word in a dictionary. Write the correct definition on the line.*

When you look up a word in the dictionary, always make sure you are looking at the correct part of speech.

noun   verb   1. If you **charge** too much on your credit card, it may be hard to pay the bill.

_____

noun   verb   2. Can you **check** the price of these jeans?

_____

noun   verb   3. The shirt doesn't fit, so I plan to **return** it.

_____

noun   verb   4. Jim checked the **balance** in his checking account to make sure he had enough money to pay his phone bill.

_____

noun   verb   5. The credit counselor helped me set up a **budget**.

_____

9. Multiple-Meaning Words

Some words have more than one meaning. To figure out the correct meaning, look at how the word is used in the sentence. You can also look at nearby words for clues.

Look at the underlined word. Circle the letter of the best definition.

1. The <u>sign</u> in the window says that the store doesn't accept checks.
   a. a notice with writing
   b. to write your name

2. Denny paid for lunch with a $20 <u>bill</u>.
   a. an amount of money owed for goods or services
   b. a piece of paper money

3. Some credit card companies charge 15% <u>interest</u>.
   a. a charge for borrowing money or for a loan
   b. a feeling of wanting to know more about something

4. A good cashier counts the <u>change</u> carefully before giving it to a customer.
   a. to become different
   b. the money customers get back if they pay more than they owe

Unit 7 Review

Complete each paragraph. Use words from the lists.

checkout lines	convenient	credit card	online shopping	purchases

I think it's interesting that people shop in different ways. Paul likes (1) _____ because he can

shop from home any time he wants. Paul thinks it's more (2) _____ than shopping at the

mall. At the mall, Paul sometimes has to wait in long (3) _____. At home, Paul can just type

in his (4) _____ number and address. He knows that his (5) _____ will

soon arrive at his door.

advertisement	clearance sale	discount	exchange	receipt	salesperson

Paul's sister Julia likes to shop a different way. She loves to visit the mall. Just last week her favorite store sent her

an (6) _____ in the mail. The store was having a (7) _____ on winter

clothing. All winter clothing was 50% off. At the store, Julia asked a (8) _____ to help her

find the right size. Julia paid $60 for her new coat after she got the 50% (9) _____. She saved

her (10) _____ just in case she wanted to (11) _____ the coat for a

different color.

cashier	insert	scan	self-checkout

At some large stores, you can pay for your purchases in two different ways. If you use

(12) _____, you do all the work. You (13) _____ your own items

and put them into bags. Then you pay. To pay, you (14) _____ your credit card or cash

into the machine. The machines don't take checks. If you want to pay by check, you need to go to a line with a

(15) _____.

Read each question. Then circle the correct answer.

1. **Which of these words means "the action or process of being employed"?**

   A employee

   B employer

   C employment

   D unemployed

2. **What does the word *scan* mean in this passage?**

   The cashier tried to <u>scan</u> the price tag on the shirt. But her machine could not read the information. The cashier had to enter the information from the price tag.

   A to look at quickly

   B to use a machine to collect information

   C a picture of a body part taken in a medical office

   D an image taken on a computer

3. **Which of these words means "to look at ahead of time"?**

   A preorder

   B reorder

   C preview

   D review

4. **What does the word *swipe* mean in this sentence?**

   Marco had to <u>swipe</u> his credit card several times because the card reader wasn't working.

   A steal

   B borrow

   C find

   D slide

5. **Which choice is an example of a type of *identification*?**

   A a checkbook

   B a driver's license

   C a checkout line

   D a refund

6. **Which word from the passage means about the same as *budget*?**

   Each month Linda and Joe <u>budget</u> carefully. They start by writing down how much money they make. Then they list what they must pay for housing, cell phones, transportation, and food. They plan how to spend the money they have left. They never spend more than they have.

   A start

   B pay

   C plan

   D spend

7. **Which word correctly completes the sentence?**

   When you pay with a _____, you must write the amount of your purchase in words and in numbers.

   A charge

   B bill

   C change

   D check

8. **What is the meaning of the word *bills* in this sentence?**

   Jamie used bills and coins to pay for her purchase.

   A lists or documents showing how much you owe

   B written ideas for new laws

   C pieces of paper money

   D birds' beaks

Write about an interesting or unusual experience you had shopping. Write your answer on a separate sheet of paper. Use at least six words you learned in this unit. Circle the vocabulary words you use.

Check your answers on page 106.

8 Visiting a Doctor

VOCABULARY

Read these words from the passage. Check the words you know.

- ☐ annual
- ☐ appointment
- ☐ complicated
- ☐ copayment
- ☐ diagnose
- ☐ disease
- ☐ examine
- ☐ medical
- ☐ prescription
- ☐ prevent
- ☐ specialist
- ☐ symptom

Abbreviations

M.D. (doctor of medicine)

Dr. (doctor)

ER (emergency room)

OR (operating room)

RN (registered nurse)

ICU (Intensive Care Unit)

Taking care of your body and your health is important. You already know that you should see a doctor if you are sick. But seeing a doctor for a regular checkup is also a good idea.

A Regular Checkup

Most people should have an **annual** visit with a doctor. During this **appointment**, a doctor can check your health and identify problems before they become serious. The doctor might also give you advice about how to be healthy.

When you go for a regular checkup, the doctor's office will usually get a **medical** history. They will ask about any **diseases** or health conditions you or members of your family have. They will also ask about any medications you take.

During the checkup, the doctor will **examine** different parts of your body. She might order lab tests. After the examination, the doctor will recommend some ways to **prevent** illness and stay healthy. Your doctor might suggest that you:

- get enough sleep.
- maintain a healthy weight.
- stop smoking.
- exercise regularly.

When You Are Sick

If you are sick, see a doctor right away. At your appointment, the doctor or nurse will ask about your **symptoms**. This can help them **diagnose** your illness or injury. Depending on what is wrong, they might order tests.

A doctor might also write a **prescription** to treat your illness. The doctor might send you to a **specialist** who knows more about your condition.

Using Insurance

Medical care can be expensive, so most people need health insurance. Many jobs provide health insurance, or you can buy it on your own. Before your appointment, the doctor's office will ask for your insurance card. You may have to pay a set amount for an office visit. This is called a copay, or **copayment**. Insurance can be **complicated**, so make sure you understand how your plan works.

What other health care words do you know? Write them here.

_____   _____   _____

1. Vocabulary Focus

Write the word next to its definition.

annual	appointment	complicated	copayment
diagnose	disease	examine	medical
prescription	prevent	specialist	symptom

_____ 1. to find out what kind of illness someone has

_____ 2. to stop something from happening

_____ 3. happening one time per year

_____ 4. an amount set by your insurance company that you pay for a service in a doctor's office

_____ 5. a change in your body that shows you are sick

_____ 6. to look at closely and carefully

_____ 7. a plan to meet at a certain time and place

_____ 8. a person who is an expert and knows a lot about a subject

_____ 9. a medicine that a doctor orders for a sick person

_____ 10. related to medicine and connected to treating illness

_____ 11. difficult to understand or explain

_____ 12. an illness

2. Use the Vocabulary

Describe a time when you went to the doctor. Use at least three vocabulary words. Underline the vocabulary words you use.

_____

_____

_____

_____

_____

_____

3. Work With New Vocabulary

Write your answers. Then, compare answers with a partner.

1. Give three examples of things that you need an **appointment** for.

   _____

We use shortened forms of many words.

Exam is a short form of *examination*.

Lab is a short form of *laboratory*.

Copay is a short form of *copayment*.

2. How is a **copayment** different from the regular price of a doctor's office visit?

   _____

3. Why is getting your **medical** history helpful to doctors?

   _____

4. How can you **prevent** getting a cold or the flu?

   _____

5. Why does a doctor **examine** someone?

   _____

6. Besides people, what other living things can get **diseases**?

   _____

7. What are some things you do on an **annual** basis?

   _____

Sometimes the symbol ℞ is used to stand for the word prescription.

8. Why does a doctor write a **prescription**? How can a **prescription** help you?

   _____

9. Describe the **symptoms** a person might have if he or she is sick.

   _____

10. For a checkup, should you see your regular doctor or a **specialist**? Explain why.

    _____

11. What are some ways a doctor might **diagnose** an illness?

    _____

12. Describe a time when you learned to do something **complicated**.

    _____

4. Prefix *dis-*

The prefix *dis-* can mean "not" or "the opposite of." For example, *dislike* means "to not like."

Use words from the list to complete the sentences. Check a dictionary if you don't know the meaning of a word.

disabled	disagree	discovered	disease	disturb

1. Doctors _____ about the best way to lose weight. Each one seems to have a different idea.

2. Janet needs to rest, so please don't _____ her. Don't make a lot of noise.

3. The medical researcher _____ a new way to treat the illness.

4. Heart _____ causes the highest number of deaths each year in the U.S.

5. Josef is a nurse who cares for sick and _____ people.

5. Suffixes *-ion* and *-tion*

The suffixes *-ion* and *-tion* mean "the act or process of." Many words that end in *ion* or *tion* are nouns.

Use words from the list to complete the sentences. Check a dictionary if you don't know the meaning of a word.

confusion	examination	infection	medication
operation	suggestions	vaccinations	vision

1. Don wears glasses because he has poor _____.

2. Children must get their _____ before they can attend school.

3. There is a lot of _____ about how health insurance works. It's hard to figure out.

4. The doctor told William to take the _____ twice a day.

5. Kurt needed an _____ to fix his heart problem.

6. The dentist did a careful _____ of Pete's teeth to check for any problems.

7. Bruce asked his doctor for _____ for how to lose weight.

8. Connie got an _____ in her finger. It was red and sore.

> To figure out the meaning of a word that ends in *ion* or *tion*, use what you know about the root or base word. For example, look at the word *examination*. You know that the verb *examine* means "to look at closely." So you can guess that the word *examination* means "the process of being looked at closely."

6. Compound Words

Think about the meaning of each part of a compound word.

Complete the sentences. Use words from the list.

checkup	drugstore	eye doctor	headache	office visit

1. Meg needed new glasses, so she went to see the _____.

2. Glenn gets a _____ once a year to make sure he is healthy.

3. Daniel's insurance charges a $25 copayment for an _____ with a doctor.

4. At the _____ you can get prescriptions and other medications.

5. Valerie woke up with a bad _____. The pain was terrible, so she took an aspirin.

7. Context Clues: Examples and General Clues

The words *for example, such as, including,* and *for instance* are clues that a writer is giving examples.

● **Look for hints and clues to figure out words you don't know. Sometimes you can look for words and ideas that are examples of an unknown word.**

Underline examples that help explain each boldfaced word. Then write a definition for the word.

1. My doctor gave me two pieces of **advice**. She said I should get seven hours of sleep each night and lose some weight.

   _____

2. After the accident, Raymundo had several **injuries**, including a cut, a broken bone, and a bruise.

   _____

In the word *pharmacy,* the letters *ph* make the *f* sound. The first part of *pharmacy* sounds like *farm.*

● 3. Sofia took Roberto to the **pharmacy** to get the medication his doctor prescribed.

   _____

4. Smoking can be harmful to **organs** such as the heart, lungs, and even the stomach.

   _____

5. Being overweight can cause **complications** like breathing problems and heart disease.

   _____

6. People in Dina's family have serious health **conditions**. For example, Dora's mom has heart disease, and her dad has diabetes.

   _____

8. Parts of Speech and the Dictionary

To figure out the meaning of a word, look at how it is used in the sentence.

Look up each boldfaced word in a dictionary. Write a definition that matches how the word is used in the sentence.

1. I called my health insurance company to see if it will **cover** my treatment.

   _____

2. Becky's doctor will **order** a blood test.

   _____

3. Andrew got a **shot** to prevent the flu.

   _____

4. You can **fill** your prescription at the pharmacy on Oak Street.

   _____

9. Multiple-Meaning Words

Many words can have more than one meaning.

In each of these sentences, the same word has two different meanings. Think about how each word is used. Then use a dictionary to look up definitions. Write the definitions on the line.

1. The doctor was 30 minutes late, so the nurse asked the <u>patient</u> to be <u>patient</u>.

a.   b.

   a. _____

   b. _____

2. The <u>body</u> of knowledge about the human <u>body</u> has increased greatly in the last 100 years.

a.   b.

   a. _____

   b. _____

3. Don't eat too many <u>treats</u>, or a doctor may need to <u>treat</u> you for being overweight.

a.   b.

   a. _____

   b. _____

4. During Jordan's annual <u>physical</u>, her doctor checked her <u>physical</u> appearance.

a.   b.

   a. _____

   b. _____

5. The doctors in that office <u>care</u> about the kind of <u>care</u> they give.

a.   b.

   a. _____

   b. _____

Unit 8 Review

Read about Julie's trip to the doctor. Complete the sentences with words from the list.

appointment	examination	headaches	infection
pharmacy	prescribe	symptoms	vision

Julie wasn't feeling well. She decided to make an (1) _____ to see her doctor. Dr. Patel asked Julie to describe her (2) _____.

"Well, I can't see very clearly. My (3) _____ is a little blurry. I also have bad (4) _____. The pain in my head just won't go away," Julie said.

Dr. Patel gave Julie a careful (5) _____. She checked her eyes, nose, ears, and throat. She also did some tests.

"It looks like you have an (6) _____. I am going to (7) _____ some medicine. Take the medicine twice a day with food. You should feel better in two to three days," Dr. Patel said.

After Julie left the doctor's office, she went to the (8) _____ right away to get the medicine. She wanted to feel better as soon as possible.

Read this information about influenza, or the flu, an illness that can be serious. Complete the sentences with words from the list.

complications	conditions	medical	prescription	prevent
recommendations	shot	treat	vaccination	

Flu Facts

The flu can be a serious illness. It is caused by a virus. It spreads easily from person to person. The best way to (9) _____ the flu is by getting the flu vaccine. (10) _____ is quick and easy. You can get flu vaccine two ways. The most common way is in a (11) _____. If you are afraid of needles, you can also get the vaccine in a nose spray.

Who should get the vaccine?

Everyone should get the vaccine. But the young and old really need it. They can have serious (12) _____ if they get the flu. For example, they can have breathing problems or get infections.

People with health (13) _____ such as heart problems should also get the vaccine. The flu can make them very sick.

What should you do if you get the flu?

If you get the flu, talk to your doctor right away. Your doctor might give you a (14) _____ that helps (15) _____ the flu. Your doctor might also make some (16) _____ for things you can do at home, such as drink a lot of liquids and get lots of rest. Most people get better in a couple of weeks on their own. Other people, though, may need (17) _____ care.

Read each question. Then circle the correct answer.

1. **Which definition of *cover* matches the meaning in this passage?**

   Walter wants to stop smoking. His insurance plan will <u>cover</u> the cost of his treatment.

   A to place over

   B to pay for

   C to report a news event

   D to travel a distance

2. **Which word correctly completes the passage?**

   Mrs. Li went to the pharmacy. She needed to pick up some _____.

   A operations

   B infections

   C complications

   D medications

3. **Which word best completes the passage?**

   Ben is very _____. He forgets about his appointments and often loses his keys and cell phone.

   A disorganized

   B organization

   C organizer

   D reorganize

4. **What does the word *diagnose* mean in this sentence?**

   The doctor used a test to <u>diagnose</u> Oscar's illness.

   A to stop something from happening

   B to make something more difficult

   C to look at carefully

   D to find out what is making someone sick

5. **What does the word *patient* mean in this sentence?**

   Dr. Ruiz helped her <u>patient</u> lose weight.

   A a place where you can buy medicine

   B a place where you can go if you are very sick

   C a person who gets medical care

   D a person who knows a lot about a certain kind of medicine

6. **Which word from the passage means about the same as *disease*?**

   Rose had a long illness when she was a child. She had a kind of heart <u>disease</u>. When she got older, she had an operation. Her health improved.

   A illness

   B child

   C operation

   D health

7. **If you go for an *annual* visit to your doctor, how often do you go?**

   A once a day

   B once a week

   C once a month

   D once a year

8. **Which of the following best completes the passage?**

   Roger hurt his knee. His doctor said he should see _____ in knee problems.

   A an eye doctor

   B an organ

   C a specialist

   D a patient

Why are regular checkups important? Write your answer on a separate sheet of paper. Use at least six words you learned in this unit. Circle the vocabulary words you use.

Check your answers beginning on page 106.

9 Shopping for Healthy Food

VOCABULARY

Read these words from the passage. Check the words you know.

- [ ] aisles
- [ ] experts
- [ ] facts
- [ ] impulse
- [ ] ingredients
- [ ] items
- [ ] label
- [ ] nutritionists
- [ ] packaged
- [ ] perimeter
- [ ] processed
- [ ] produce

Abbreviations

FDA (Food and Drug Administration)

GMO (genetically modified organism)

g (grams)

mg (milligrams)

The way you walk around the grocery store can change the way you eat.

Living a healthy life includes making healthy choices when you're shopping for food. Close your eyes for one minute and picture the grocery store or supermarket where you usually shop. Where is all of the fresh food? Where are the **produce** section, the meat and seafood departments, and the dairy case? Most likely they are located around the outside **perimeter** of the store. The outer **aisles** of a grocery store are usually where you find the freshest food. **Nutritionists** say that you should spend most of your food shopping time in the outer aisles. The food there is generally more natural and healthier than the **packaged** foods you find in the middle aisles.

There are healthy **items**, such as tuna, canned beans, and brown rice, in the middle aisles of most grocery stores. In general; however, the food there is more likely to be **processed** and less nutritious than the food on the perimeter. So read the **label** on the back of the packaging. Understanding the nutrition **facts** can help you make educated food choices. Look carefully at the **ingredients**. The fewer ingredients, the better. Some **experts** say that if you can't pronounce the ingredients listed on the outside of a package, you probably shouldn't eat the food inside it.

Make a shopping list and organize it by where the items are located in your market. For example, list all the fruits and vegetables together and all dairy products together. And never shop on an empty stomach. You're more likely to keep to a healthy eating plan and less likely to make an **impulse** purchase if you have a well-organized list and are not hungry when you get to the store.

Do you know any other words about shopping to stay healthy? Write them here.

_____ _____ _____

1. Vocabulary Focus

Write the word next to its definition.

aisle	experts	facts	impulse
ingredient	items	label	nutritionists
packaged	perimeter	processed	produce

When the word *produce* is a noun, say PROduce. When *produce* is a verb, say proDUCE.

_____ 1. fruits and vegetables

_____ 2. a sudden strong wish to do something

_____ 3. a piece of paper or material attached to something to describe it

_____ 4. an open space to walk between rows of shelves

_____ 5. boxed, bagged, canned, or jarred

_____ 6. single things in a list or series

_____ 7. people who know a great deal about a particular thing

_____ 8. the outer boundary of an area

_____ 9. things that are said or known to be true

_____ 10. people who are trained in the science of food and health

_____ 11. changed by a special treatment

_____ 12. one of the parts of a mixture

2. Use the Vocabulary

Choose three of the vocabulary words. Define them in your own words.

1. _____

2. _____

3. _____

Share your definitions with a partner. Talk about them, and make suggestions for revising them. Rewrite your definitions and show them to your teacher.

3. Work With New Vocabulary

Write your answers. Then compare answers with a partner.

1. What **processed** foods do you buy most often?

_____

2. What things do you think people buy on **impulse** when they're grocery shopping?

_____

3. Why do you think food companies are required to list the **ingredients** on food labels?

_____

4. From which supermarket **aisles** do you buy the most food?

_____

5. What are some different ways food can be **packaged**?

_____

6. If you had to make a shopping list right now, what four **items** you would start with?

_____

7. What area would you like to be an **expert** in? Why?

_____

8. Name three places where a **nutritionist** might find a job.

_____

9. What do you notice first when you see the **label** on a can or box of food?

_____

10. Why do you think the fresh food is usually on the **perimeter** of a supermarket?

_____

11. What three things in the **produce** section do you buy most often?

_____

12. What **fact** from the article about shopping for healthy food did you think was most interesting? Explain your answer.

_____

4. Prefixes *in-* and *im-*

When *in-* and *im-* are at the beginning of a word, they can mean "in" or "into." For example,
inhale **means "to breathe in."**

Match the word with its definition. Write the correct letter.

_____ 1. inform   a. something brought in from another country to sell

_____ 2. install   b. the part near the middle of something

_____ 3. immigrate   c. to put a new thing in place so it is ready to use

_____ 4. inside   d. to come to live in a country after leaving your own

_____ 5. import   e. to tell someone something

● Don't be fooled by words that begin with *in-* or *im-* but do not use a prefix (*inch*).

● Use the prefix *im-* when a root or base word starts with the letter *b, m,* or *p.*

5. Suffix *-er*

You know that when the suffix *-er* is added to some nouns, it can mean "a person who." When the suffix *-er* is added to an adjective, it compares two things and means "more." For example,
smart + -er = smarter. **An educated shopper is a smarter shopper.**

Rewrite the words below. Add -er.

1. big _____   4. healthy _____

2. close _____   5. hungry _____

3. fresh _____

Check your answers for the questions above. Then use the words to complete the sentences below.

6. The _____ you are when you're grocery shopping, the more likely you are to buy impulse items.

7. Travis is living a _____ life than he used to. He eats more fruits and vegetables and tries to avoid processed foods.

8. Food stores come in all sizes. Supermarkets are generally _____ than grocery stores.

9. Which supermarket is _____ to Mario's home—the one on Woodward Road or the one on Coro Street?

10. The produce at Bigtop Market is usually _____ than the produce at Peter's Groceries.

● For adjectives that end in a consonant + *y*, change *y* to *i* and add *-er.*
funny/funnier

For adjectives that end in a consonant + vowel + consonant, double the last consonant and add *-er.*
hot/hotter

For adjectives that end with a silent *e*, drop the *e* and add *-er.*
large/larger

6. Compound Words

When you don't know if a compound word is one word, two words, three words, or hyphenated, look it up in a dictionary. If you can't find an entry for the compound, treat it as separate words.

Write the compound word that matches the clue.

bulk food	expiration date	whole grain

1. _____: the month and year after which processed food cannot be sold

2. _____: food that is made from unprocessed grain

3. _____: food that is sold in large unpackaged amounts

Complete each sentence with a compound word. Use a dictionary to check the meaning of a word if you need to.

farmers' market	shopping carts	store brands	weekly specials

4. Henry and Jeannie shop at the _____ every Saturday morning. They like buying directly from local food growers.

5. Supermarkets make their _____ large so that people will buy more food.

6. Read the newspaper to find out what the _____ are at different markets in your neighborhood. Then you can shop for the things you want at the best price.

7. Experts recommend buying _____. They're less expensive, and the food usually tastes just as good as big-name items.

7. Context Clues: Definitions and Synonyms

Sometimes difficult words are defined in a text. You can also look for synonyms, words with similar meanings.

Read each sentence. Look for clues to help you understand the meaning of the boldfaced word. Write the meaning on the line.

1. Most farmers' markets have a large **selection** of fresh produce. There are always a lot of things to choose from.

   A *selection* is _____

2. More than half of the food that Americans **consume**, or buy and use, is processed.

   To *consume* means _____

3. **Avoid** processed and sugary foods. Stay away from unhealthy food choices.

   Avoid means _____

4. Shopping the perimeter of a market is part of a life plan to **prevent**, or stop, heart disease.

   To *prevent* means _____

8. Parts of Speech and the Dictionary

To figure out the meaning of a word, look at how it is used in the sentence.

Look up each boldfaced word in a dictionary. Write the definition that matches how the word is used in the sentence.

1. Those stores **market** to people who are interested in food that has not been processed.

   _____

2. A farmer's goal is to **produce** good food in order to make a living.

   _____

3. Do you try to eat a healthy **diet**?

   _____

4. People who shop at farmers' markets think it's important to **shop** locally.

   _____

5. You **bag** your own food when you buy in bulk.

   _____

9. Multiple-Meaning Words

Some words have more than one meaning. To figure out the correct meaning, look at how the word is used in the sentence. You can also look at nearby words for clues.

Look at each underlined word. Circle the letter of the best definition.

1. Do you think that some food, like milk, is better for you when it's <u>processed</u>?
   a. straightened
   b. been through a special chemical procedure

2. Fresh food and <u>staples</u> are usually located on the outside aisles or at the far end of the store.
   a. pieces of wire pushed through papers and bent to hold them together
   b. main or basic things

3. My neighbors have a <u>store</u> of food and water in case of an emergency.
   a. a place where things are bought and sold
   b. things that you are keeping to use later

4. The food at that market is always fresh. Local farmers <u>deliver</u> new produce almost every day.
   a. to take something to the place where it must go
   b. to give birth to a baby

5. The dairy <u>case</u> isn't working again. I wonder what's wrong with it.
   a. a crime that police must solve
   b. a container to keep something in

Complete the paragraphs. Use words from the lists.

facts	ingredients	labels	nutritionists	packaged	produce

This list for shopping to stay healthy was written by two (1) _____ who spoke at Gary's life-skills class last week.

A Healthy Diet

▲ Stay away from (2) _____ food. The more packaging, the less healthy the food probably is for you.

▲ Read the nutrition (3) _____ on cans, boxes, and bags of food completely. Don't buy anything that has (4) _____ you've never heard of.

▲ Half of what you eat should be (5) _____. Eating a variety of bright and colorful fruits and vegetables is an easy and delicious way to get the nutrition your body needs.

▲ Go to www.fitness.gov for more helpful (6) _____ and information about staying healthy and keeping fit.

aisles	experts	impulse	items	perimeter	processed

▲ Avoid the supermarket (7) _____ with sugary drinks and soda. (8) _____ market those drinks so that you want to buy them. And nothing about those sweet (9) _____ is good for you.

▲ Supermarket managers carefully place a lot of delicious-looking (10) _____ food near the cash registers. They are hoping you will make an (11) _____ purchase while you are waiting in line.

▲ And always shop the (12) _____ to find the best food for you, your friends, and your family.

Read each question. Then circle the correct answer.

1. **What does the word *impress* mean in this sentence?**

   All of the colorful fruits and vegetables at Frank's Market <u>impress</u> me every time I'm there. They make me want to buy one of everything.

   A to leave a lasting effect

   B to use pressure to leave a mark

   C to stress something to a person

   D to press down on something

2. **Which word best completes the sentence?**

   Ari likes to shop at the new supermarket because it is _____ than the old market.

   A cleaned

   B cleanly

   C cleaner

   D cleaning

3. **Which of these compound words means "food that is sold in large unpackaged amounts"?**

   A store brand

   B weekly special

   C bulk food

   D farmers' market

4. **Which of the following is an example of *produce*?**

   A a can of beans

   B a bunch of grapes

   C a bag of potato chips

   D a box of pasta

5. **Which word best completes the passage?**

   Next time you're out shopping, look around you. Most stores are designed to encourage _____ shopping.

   A processed

   B packaged

   C impulse

   D item

6. **Which of these compound words describes a food that uses all parts of a grain like wheat or oats?**

   A bulk food

   B store brands

   C expiration date

   D whole grain

7. **Which definition of *fit* matches the meaning in this question?**

   Does Raymond's new suit still <u>fit</u> since he started his diet?

   A good enough

   B in good health

   C to be the right shape and size for

   D to put something into place

8. **Which word best completes the passage?**

   Most experts tell us to stay away from the middle aisles of the supermarket. They say it's an easy way to _____ buying processed food.

   A inform

   B avoid

   C consume

   D shop

What advice about grocery shopping would you give a young person who was living on his or her own for the first time? Write your answer on a separate sheet of paper. Use at least six words you learned in this unit. Circle the vocabulary words you use.

Check your answers on page 107.

10 Protecting Personal Information Online

VOCABULARY

Read these words from the passage. Check the words you know.

- ☐ access
- ☐ characters
- ☐ crime
- ☐ data
- ☐ email
- ☐ identity theft
- ☐ laptop
- ☐ message
- ☐ multiple
- ☐ online
- ☐ password
- ☐ protect

Abbreviations

FTC (Federal Trade Commission)

IM (instant messaging)

SSN (Social Security number)

Do you know how to stay safe and protect your personal information on the Internet?

The Internet can make life easy. With **laptops** and smartphones, you can **access** just about anything you want at any time and in any place. You can take an **online** class, send an instant **message**, buy a great pair of pants, or deposit your paycheck.

Life has also become a little more dangerous because of the Internet. The personal information that you share can open you to **identity theft**.

When you use the Internet, **protect** your personal information. Here are some ways to do that:

- If you use a credit card for online shopping, watch your account activity. If you see purchases that you haven't made, contact the credit card company right away.

- Choose passwords that are hard to figure out. When you create passwords, use letters, numbers, and **characters** like %, *, and @. Make your password at least eight characters long because longer passwords are harder for others to guess or steal. Don't use your name, your birthday, or your address in your password. Also avoid patterns like "12341234."

- Protect your **passwords**. Don't use the same password for **multiple** accounts. That way, even if someone figures out one password, he or she can't access your other accounts. Store your passwords in a safe place. It can be hard to remember all of them, so you may want to make a list. Keep that list in a safe place and separate from your computer.

- Don't reply to any **emails** that ask you to provide personal **data** like credit card account numbers, your Social Security number, or your account password. The messages may appear to be from a bank or other company you do business with. Honest companies never contact you in this way or ask for additional personal information.

The FBI says that identity theft is America's fastest growing **crime** problem. Protect your money and yourself. If you think that someone has stolen your identity, contact the FTC (Federal Trade Commission).

Do you know any other words about protecting your personal information online? Write them here.

_____ _____ _____

1. Vocabulary Focus

Write the word next to its definition.

access	character	crime	data
email	identity theft	laptop	message
multiple	online	password	protect

_____ 1. something that someone does that is against the law

_____ 2. a small secret set of letters and symbols that allows you to access a computer

_____ 3. written information sent from one person or group to another

_____ 4. accessed through the Internet

_____ 5. more than one

_____ 6. a small computer that is easy to carry

_____ 7. to get to information, especially on a computer

_____ 8. a crime in which someone uses another person's personal information to get credit cards, goods, or money

_____ 9. a message written on one computer and sent to another

_____ 10. a printed letter or symbol

_____ 11. facts or information

_____ 12. to keep something or someone safe

2. Use the Vocabulary

Choose three of the vocabulary words. Define them in your own words.

1. _____

2. _____

3. _____

Share your definitions with a partner. Talk about them, and make suggestions for revising them. Rewrite your definitions and show them to your teacher.

3. Work With New Vocabulary

Write your answers. Then compare answers with a partner.

1. How many **characters** are there in the password you use most often?

   _____

2. What is the **email** address you write to most often?

   _____

3. Name a good place to keep your **passwords**.

   _____

4. What are the advantages of using a **laptop**?

   _____

5. Why do you think **identity theft** is such a fast-growing crime?

   _____

6. How much time do you spend **online** each day?

   _____

7. What do you do to protect yourself against **crime**?

   _____

8. What personal **data** would you never share with anyone?

   _____

9. Who do you get the most **messages** from?

   _____

10. Who has **access** to your passwords?

    _____

11. How do you **protect** the things you own?

    _____

12. You can have **multiple** online accounts. What other things do people have in multiples?

    _____

4. Prefixes *em–*, *en–*

The prefixes *em–* and *en–* mean "to cause to" or "to provide with something."

Read each word and its definition. Then use the word in a sentence.

1. endanger: to cause someone or something to be in danger

   _____

2. empower: to give someone the power to do something

   _____

3. enjoy: to get pleasure or joy from something

   _____

4. encourage: to give someone support or courage to do something

   _____

5. employ: to give someone a job

   _____

6. enable: to make possible or easy

   _____

> The prefix *em–* is used when a word or root starts with *b*, *m*, or *p*. The prefix *en–* is used before words or roots that start with other letters.

Exercise 5 Root *port*

The root *port* means "to carry."

Use a word from the list to complete each sentence. Check a dictionary if you don't know the meaning of a word.

imported	portable	portfolio	report	support	transportation

1. A flash drive is a _____ device that you can store computer data on.

2. Some forms of public _____ now have free Internet access.

3. Reggie _____ all the data from his old computer to his new laptop.

4. The company offers six months of free phone _____ if customers want help with their new computers.

5. If someone steals your identity, _____ it to the police right away.

6. Carlos made a _____ of all his art projects for class.

> The word *port* can mean a place on a computer where you connect other devices, such as printers or monitors.

6. Compound Words

If the dictionary doesn't have an entry for a compound word, the compound is probably written as two separate words.

Remember, the second part of a compound word usually carries most of the meaning. For example, a *mouse pad* is a pad to put under a computer mouse.

Complete each sentence. Use a word from the list.

download	keyboard	search engine	smartphone	user name

1. Try to find a _____ that meets your needs and is comfortable to type on. Elizabeth bought one that is lightweight, wireless, and washable!

2. Don't _____ free software from the Internet unless you are familiar with the company and know that it is both good and secure.

3. Your _____ is your online identity. You have to choose one whenever you open a new account.

4. A _____ can do almost everything a computer can do. And it fits in your pocket!

5. A _____ helps you find information on the web. Some are designed just for kids, and others are designed for people with lots of experience using the web.

7. Context Clues: Definitions and General Clues

When you read an unfamiliar word, you can check to see if the writer has explained it. You can also look at surrounding words for clues about it.

The word *blog* is a short form of the words *web log*.

attachment	blog	monitor	security	socialize	vulnerable

Complete each sentence. Use a word from the list.

1. Don't reuse the same password for multiple accounts. It makes all of those accounts _____. They can be more easily attacked if your password is discovered.

2. An email _____ is a document or file that is sent with an email message. It can be any type of file.

3. Justin is studying computer _____ at college. He's interested in the protection of computing systems and the data they store.

4. Some people _____ online for hours every day. They share photos, information, news, and ideas on places like Twitter, Facebook, Pinterest, and Instagram.

5. Instead of writing in a journal, Trudy writes an online _____ about fashion, gardening, motorcycles, and all the other things that interest her.

6. Alcott Industries uses software to _____ how its employees use their time online. The software checks how long they spend online and what websites they visit.

8. Parts of Speech and the Dictionary

To figure out the meaning of a word, look at how it is used in the sentence.

Look up each boldfaced word in a dictionary. Write the definition that matches how the word is used in the sentence.

1. Acme Supermarket is going to **post** job openings on their website.

   _____

2. When you download **files**, make sure they come from sources you can trust.

   _____

3. How many names do you have in the **contact** list on your phone?

   _____

4. Karen likes to **reply** to all of her emails at the same time.

   _____

5. Experts recommend that you **separate** your personal emails from your business emails.

   _____

9. Multiple-Meaning Words

Some words have more than one meaning. To figure out the correct meaning, look at how the word is used in the sentence. Look also at nearby words for clues.

Look at each underlined word. Circle the letter of the best definition.

1. After the fire at the community center, there was a lot of **activity** on the city website.
   a. a lot of people doing a lot of things
   b. something that you do because you enjoy it

2. Lee was feeling tired and accidently downloaded a **virus**.
   a. a very small living thing that causes a disease
   b. a hidden program that stops your computer from working correctly

3. Toni wrote about two main **characters**—a little boy and his friend Jake.
   a. a letter, number, or symbol that is written, printed, or used in computer programs
   b. people in books, TV shows, movies, etc.

4. Lin's job is to **scan** all of the photos in the book.
   a. to read something quickly
   b. to use a piece of equipment to copy and store information on a computer

5. After Lin scans the photos, he has to **save** them online.
   a. to store information on a computer
   b. to use less of

Unit 10 Review

Read about how the Davila family uses technology. Complete the paragraph with words from the list.

| blogs | keyboard | laptop | online | reports | smartphone | socialize |

In the Davila household, everyone loves technology. In fact, it's common for all four people to be

(1) _____ at the same time, each using a different device. Mr. Davila uses a desktop

computer. Sometimes he does office work, such as writing (2) _____, at home. But he also

likes to read the news. Mrs. Davila uses a (3) _____ computer. She likes it because she can

use it anywhere in the house. She often reads cooking (4) _____ to get recipe ideas. Julio

Davila uses a tablet. It doesn't have a (5) _____, but it does have a touch screen. Julio uses it

to stream movies and videos. April Davila uses the smallest device, a (6) _____. She doesn't

use it to make calls, though. She uses it to (7) _____ with her friends from school and spends

a lot of time texting every night. It's a good thing the Davilas have unlimited Internet usage at home.

Read about a company's rules for using the Internet. Complete the paragraph with the words from the list.

| contact | data | download | email | encourage |
| enforcing | messages | monitor | password | viruses |

The C&E Company sent this memo to its employees:

MEMO: Rules for Using the Internet at C&E Company

C&E Company wants to keep its computer system safe, so we have written a new set of rules for using the
Internet at work. We (8) _____ you to read and understand the rules. You should
(9) _____ human resources if you have any questions or concerns. We will be
(10) _____ these new rules and policies starting September 1. Employees will get written
warnings if they break the rules.

• Every worker will need a user name and (11) _____ in order to log into the computer system.
  You will need to change your password every 90 days.

• Use your company (12) _____ account for company business only. Don't use your company
  address to send personal (13) _____ to friends and family or for shopping.

• Use the Internet responsibly while you are at work. We use software to (14) _____ Internet
  use on company computers. The software blocks you from going to unsafe web pages.

• Don't (15) _____ software, games, or pictures onto your company computer. They may
  contain (16) _____ that could damage your computer. They could also contain harmful
  programs that could steal company (17) _____.

Read each question. Then circle the correct answer.

1. **Which definition of *character* matches the meaning in this passage?**

   Rona's bank has rules about passwords. Passwords must include at least one special <u>character</u>, one capital letter, and one number.

   A a person or animal in a book or movie

   B an interesting or unusual person

   C the way that something is

   D a sign, mark, or symbol

2. **Which word best completes the sentence?**

   People can _____ the Internet on their smartphones.

   A protect

   B empower

   C endanger

   D access

3. **What does the word *multiple* mean in this sentence?**

   The owner needs to buy <u>multiple</u> copies of the software if he wants to put it on all of the car repair shop's computers.

   A many

   B expensive

   C current

   D safe

4. **What does the word *portable* mean in this sentence?**

   Camila wanted a <u>portable</u> computer for school, so she bought the laptop with a 10" screen instead of the one with a 17" screen.

   A easy to see

   B easy to carry

   C easy to buy

   D easy to hide

5. **Which meaning of *save* matches how the word is used in this sentence?**

   When you are writing a report on your computer, remember to <u>save</u> your work often.

   A to keep money instead of spending it

   B to avoid wasting something

   C to collect something that you want or enjoy

   D to store something safely so you can go back to it

6. **Which word from the passage means about the same as *reply*?**

   At the Benner Company, employees should answer customers' questions quickly and politely. When you receive an email asking about our products, try to <u>reply</u> within one hour. Give customers your contact information in case they have other questions.

   A answer

   B receive

   C try

   D give

7. **Which of the following helps you find information on the Internet?**

   A identify theft

   B keyboard

   C search engine

   D download

8. **Which word best completes the sentence?**

   Sheila needed help using her new computer, so she called the technical _____ number.

   A export

   B crime

   C support

   D attachment

Why is it important to be careful when using the Internet? Write your answer on a separate sheet of paper. Use at least six words you learned in this unit. Circle the vocabulary words you use.

Check your answers on page 107.

11 Getting the News

VOCABULARY

Read these words from the passage. Check the words you know.

- ☐ article
- ☐ broadcast
- ☐ cable
- ☐ current
- ☐ entertain
- ☐ inform
- ☐ issue
- ☐ local
- ☐ mass media
- ☐ print
- ☐ reporter
- ☐ section

Abbreviation

TV (television)

News is new information. There are many ways to find out what's happening in the world. How do you get the news and stay informed?

People get the news through different kinds of **mass media**. These include **print** sources, such as newspapers and magazines. People can also listen to the radio, watch TV **broadcasts**, and get news through the Internet.

Newspapers

Do you know how to find information in a newspaper? Most newspapers are organized into **sections**. The front page usually has the most important stories. Other sections might be about **local** news, sports, business, or entertainment. Besides news stories, papers have editorials. Editorials give opinions about **issues** and events rather than just facts. Some papers have columns. A column appears regularly in the paper and is usually written by the same person, or columnist.

When you look at a newspaper, you can quickly skim the headlines on a page. A headline tells the main point or focus of an **article**. The first paragraph of an article usually gives the most important facts.

TV News

Watching television news is different from reading a paper. A TV news broadcast uses video to show news. **Reporters** present the stories on live TV. Most TV news stories are short, so they give fewer details than newspaper stories. But they allow you to see things for yourself.

You can watch TV news on local stations. Local channels have stories about your area as well as national and world news. Sports and weather reports are popular parts of local news. News shows are usually 30 or 60 minutes long. Today there are also **cable** TV channels that show news 24 hours a day. Some shows on these channels are meant to **entertain** more than **inform** viewers.

Internet News

Most newspapers and TV stations have websites with **current** news. Like TV, the Internet can show news almost immediately. Websites usually have both articles and video. Computers, tablets, and smartphones allow people to see the news almost anywhere and anytime.

What other words about the news do you know? Write them here.

_____ _____ _____

1. Vocabulary Focus

Write the word next to its definition.

article	broadcast	cable	current	entertain	inform
issue	local	mass media	print	reporter	section

_____ 1. writing that has been printed, as in a newspaper or magazine

_____ 2. a television or radio program

_____ 3. to give people facts and information about a topic

_____ 4. a piece of writing in a newspaper that gives information about a topic

_____ 5. a separate part of a newspaper

_____ 6. happening now

_____ 7. having to do with a place near you

_____ 8. sources of information that reach many people, such as newspapers, radio, and television

_____ 9. a person whose job is to write or tell the news for newspapers, radio, or television

_____ 10. a system in which viewers pay to get TV through wires

_____ 11. to interest people with something they enjoy

_____ 12. an important topic that people discuss

2. Write the New Words

Are you interested in the news? Describe why or why not. Use at least three vocabulary words. Underline the vocabulary words you use.

_____

_____

_____

_____

_____

3. Work With New Vocabulary

Write your answers. Then compare answers with a partner.

The word *media* is the plural form (meaning more than one) of *medium*.

1. What are some examples of **mass media**?

   _____

2. How is a news **broadcast** different from a news article?

   _____

3. What kinds of **print** materials do you read?

   _____

4. What are the most important **issues** in the news today?

   _____

5. In what ways can you **inform** people about a topic?

   _____

6. Why do you think newspapers have different **sections**?

   _____

7. Why do newspapers and TV news shows need **reporters**?

   _____

8. Describe some stories you might read or see in **local** news.

   _____

9. Do you think TV mostly **entertains** people, or does it inform people more? Why?

   _____

We often use just the word *cable* to stand for the term *cable television*.

10. You have to pay more to get **cable** TV. Is the price worth it? Explain why.

    _____

11. What kinds of **articles** do you like to read in a newspaper?

    _____

12. If you want to find the most **current** news, would you use a newspaper, TV show, or news website? Why?

    _____

4. Roots *vis* and *vid*

The roots *vis* and *vid* mean "to see" or "to look at." For example, *visible* means "able to be seen."

Use a word from the list to complete each sentence. Check a dictionary if you don't know the meaning of a word.

revise	supervises	television	video	visible	vision

1. Mrs. Chang sits close to her TV because she has poor _____.

2. You can watch news on your _____ at any time of day or night.

3. The website has a _____ of the event and an article about it.

4. The writer had to _____ her news report when she got new information.

5. The weather report says the sky will be clear and the full moon will be _____.

6. Stan _____ the work of all the reporters at that newspaper. He is their boss.

5. Suffix *–ist*

The suffix *–ist* is found at the end of nouns that name people. The suffix *–ist* means that a person does an activity or action. For example, an *artist* is a person who makes art.

Read each word with the suffix –ist and its definition. Then use the word in a sentence.

The suffix *–ist* often follows the root *logy*, which means "the study of." For example, *geology* is the study of the earth, and a *geologist* is a person who studies the earth.

1. journalist: a person who writes news reports

_____

2. meteorologist: a person who studies the weather

_____

3. tourist: a person who visits a place for fun

_____

4. finalist: a person or team that plays in the final game

_____

5. cartoonist: a person who draws cartoons

_____

6. columnist: a person who writes a regular column for a newspaper

_____

6. Compound Words

An open compound has space between the words. In a closed compound, the words are put together. Think about the meanings of the parts of a compound word whether the words are separate or together.

Write the compound word that matches the clue.

advice column	byline	headline	press conference	TV station

1. _____ a station or company that broadcasts television shows

2. _____ a column in a newspaper that gives advice, or ideas for how to fix a problem

3. _____ a line of writing that tells who wrote an article, or who it is by

4. _____ a conference or meeting with reporters

5. _____ a line of writing that gives the title of a news article

7. Context Clues: Definitions and General Clues

Writers sometimes define or explain difficult words within sentences. Look for definitions, explanations, and other clues to figure out unknown words.

Write a definition or explanation of each boldfaced word.

The words *is, are, means,* and *refers to* can signal that a writer is defining a word.

1. **Editorials** are articles that give opinions about issues or events and are printed in a separate part of a newspaper.

   _____

2. The meteorologist gave a **forecast**, a prediction of what the weather would be like.

   _____

3. When you **skim** the news, you look quickly at the headlines and read to find main ideas.

   _____

A writer might also use commas to set off the explanation of a word or term: Newspaper delivery, **or bringing the paper to your home**, costs $25 per month.

4. A TV news **anchor**, the person who reads the news and introduces news reports, must have good communication skills.

   _____

5. **Bias** is a preset opinion about whether something is good or bad.

   _____

6. **Coverage** of the hurricane was on TV all day, and the reporting continued into the next day.

   _____

7. Donna likes to read the newspaper, but she does not want to **subscribe** to it. It costs too much to get the paper every day.

   _____

8. Parts of Speech and the Dictionary

If you need help figuring out an unknown word, think about what part of speech the word plays. For example, ask yourself if the word names something (a noun), if it tells an action (verb), or describes a noun (adjective).

Write the part of speech of the boldfaced word in each sentence. Check a dictionary if you aren't sure.

_____ 1. Anne watches a **program** that starts at 10 p.m.

_____ 2. Brian knows how to **program** the TV remote control.

_____ 3. A reporter was **present** at the event.

_____ 4. The reporter will **present** the story on the evening news.

_____ 5. A new **issue** of my favorite magazine comes out this week.

_____ 6. The president will **issue** a statement on the news tonight.

_____ 7. In my writing class, we write about **current** events.

_____ 8. The weather report says there will be a strong river **current** today.

> When *present* is used as a noun or adjective, say PREsent. When it is used as a verb, say preSENT.

9. Multiple-Meaning Words

Words can have more than one meaning. To figure out which meaning is correct, look for clues. Think about the topic and how the writer uses the word in the sentence.

Look at the underlined word. Circle the letter of the best definition.

1. Justin reads a sports <u>column</u> in the paper every Saturday.
   a. a tall post in front of a building
   b. a type of writing in a newspaper that appears regularly

2. Valeria changed the <u>channel</u> at 10 p.m. so that she could watch the news.
   a. a TV station and its programs
   b. an area of water that connects two bodies of water

3. I heard the <u>story</u> about the lost child on the morning news.
   a. a report in a newspaper or news broadcast
   b. a tale that is made up and entertains people

4. The <u>press</u> waited outside the mayor's office.
   a. a business that makes and prints books
   b. the people who write news

5. Saul prefers to get news in <u>print</u> because he likes to get more detail.
   a. writing that has been printed
   b. a copy of a painting or photo printed on paper

Unit 11 Review

Read about the Wilson family and how its members like to get their news. Complete the sentences with words from the lists.

advice column	articles	current	headlines	local	subscribe

The Wilson family likes to know what's happening in the world. They (1) _____ to

their (2) _____ newspaper. The paper gets delivered to their home every morning.

Carol Wilson likes to know about (3) _____ events, so she usually reads the

(4) _____ on the front page first. She looks at the (5) _____

to see if there's anything that interests her. After she reads the important news, Carol likes to check out the

(6) _____. She likes to read about how people can solve their problems.

column	columnist	section	skims	stories

Ryan Wilson is a sports fan. He likes to know how his favorite baseball and soccer teams are doing. He always

turns to the sports (7) _____ of the paper first. He usually (8) _____

the pages. He quickly checks to see if there are any (9) _____ about his favorite teams.

There's a sports (10) _____ Ryan likes to read, too, but it only appears on Mondays. The

(11) _____ knows a lot about baseball, and Ryan always learns something new.

cable	channel	forecast	television	video

Michelle Wilson likes sports, too. However, she prefers to get her sports news and other information from

(12) _____. She likes to see (13) _____ of the games instead of

reading articles. That way, she can see the players in action. The Wilsons have (14) _____,

so Michelle watches a (15) _____ that has sports news all day long. Michelle doesn't watch

sports all day, though. After she watches her favorite sports show, she puts on the local news. She checks out the

weather (16) _____ before she leaves for work.

Read each question. Then circle the correct answer.

1. Which definition of *print* matches the meaning in this sentence?

The city newspaper is available in <u>print</u> and online versions.

A to write separate letters by hand

B to put letters on paper using a machine

C a picture that is copied and printed on paper

D writing that is printed on paper

2. Which word correctly completes the sentence?

We watched a live _____ of the president's speech.

A byline

B broadcast

C evidence

D issue

3. Which of these words has the same meaning as *reporter*?

A journalist

B tourist

C scientist

D finalist

4. What does the word *program* mean in this sentence?

Randall watched a <u>program</u> about South America on TV last night.

A directions to make a computer do something

B a course of study

C a show that people watch on television

D a small book that gives information about a play and its actors

5. Which of the following is an example of mass media?

A a newspaper

B an article

C a reporter

D an issue

6. What does the word *meteorologist* mean in this sentence?

On the evening news, the <u>meteorologist</u> said that the weather would be cold and stormy.

A a person who writes about the same topic every week

B a person who gives their opinion about topics

C a person who reads news reports on TV

D a person who studies the weather

7. What does it mean if something is *visible*?

A You can see it.

B You can visit it.

C You can read it.

D You can pay for it.

8. Which word best completes the passage?

The TV station had good _____ of the storm. It showed video of the damage, and reporters talked to people with damaged homes.

A press

B bias

C vision

D coverage

How do you get the news? Write your answer on a separate sheet of paper. Use at least six words you learned in this unit. Circle the vocabulary words you use.

Check your answers beginning on page 107.

12 Being a Good Citizen

VOCABULARY

Read these words from the passage. Check the words you know.

- [ ] citizens
- [ ] community service
- [ ] demonstrate
- [ ] democracy
- [ ] free
- [ ] government
- [ ] limit
- [ ] responsibilities
- [ ] rights
- [ ] supported
- [ ] taxes
- [ ] vote

At one time or another, you may have thought about being a good family member, student, or worker. What does it mean to be a good citizen?

Civics is the study of **government**, history, and politics. The United States is a **democracy**. In a democracy, the people choose their leader. Since the power of the U.S. government comes from its **citizens**, it's important for you to understand your civic **rights**.

The United States is a **free** country. That means citizens have basic rights. For example, you have the right to share your ideas and thoughts on public issues with other people, including government leaders, even the president. You do this when you **vote**, but there are other things you can do as well. For example, you can send emails, speak and meet in groups, and plan and organize meetings. You can also **demonstrate** and let the government know whether you think your leaders are doing a good job. Your rights are important because they **limit** the power of the government and allow people to share ideas freely. This makes change and learning possible.

Citizens have **responsibilities** as well as rights. Some responsibilities are the things you should do, such as **community service**, or helping out your neighborhood and your neighbors. There are lots of ways to get involved—you can work with others to build a public garden, help elect a new governor, or discuss the school budget. Paying **taxes** is also a civic responsibility. Paying taxes is something you have to do, and it's not nearly as much fun as working in a garden.

The police and the courts **support** your rights and responsibilities.

Do you know any other rights or responsibilities of American citizens? Write them here.

_____   _____   _____

1. Vocabulary Focus

Match each word with its definition. Write the correct letter.

_____ 1. citizen

_____ 2. community service

_____ 3. democracy

_____ 4. demonstrate

_____ 5. free

_____ 6. government

_____ 7. limit

_____ 8. responsibility

_____ 9. right

_____ 10. support

_____ 11. tax

_____ 12. vote

a. money you have to pay the government

b. to control the size or power of something or someone

c. to make a choice in an election, to elect

d. the group of people who make laws and other important decisions for a community, state, or country

e. a freedom; something you are allowed to do by law

f. someone who was born in a country or who chose to legally belong to that country

g. to walk or stand with a group in public to show your opinions and beliefs

h. a form of government in which the people vote for their leaders

i. something you should do or have to do

j. not controlled or ruled by others

k. work that you do to help your neighborhood and the people in your neighborhood

l. to help the cause of

2. Use the Vocabulary

Choose three of the vocabulary words. Define them in your own words.

1. _____

2. _____

3. _____

Share your definitions with a partner. Talk about them, and make suggestions for revising them. Rewrite your definitions and show them to your teacher.

3. Work With New Vocabulary

Answer the questions. Then compare answers with a partner.

1. Voting is probably our most important civic right. Many young adults (18 to 24 years old) don't **vote**. Why do you think that is true?

   _____

2. Is **democracy** good for everyone and every country? Explain your answer.

   _____

3. What does it mean to you to be a good **citizen**?

   _____

4. There are many ways you can volunteer to perform **community service**. Describe something you would like to do to help your community.

   _____

5. We pay **taxes** to pay for our government. Name four things the government does with that money.

   _____

6. America is called "the land of the free." What does it mean to live in a **free** country?

   _____

7. Should you always **support** your friends? When is it OK not to support them?

   _____

8. Non-U.S. citizens have many of the same **rights** as U.S. citizens. What do you think? Should all people living in the United States have the same civic rights? Explain your answer.

   _____

9. What do you think the expression "The sky is the **limit**" means?

   _____

10. What is something you would **demonstrate** about?

    _____

11. What do you think is the most important job of our **government**?

    _____

12. Paying taxes is a civic **responsibility**. Name two personal responsibilities.

    _____

4. Prefix *un–*

The prefix *un–* means "not" or "the opposite of." *Un–* comes before a base word.

The underlined word in each sentence starts with the prefix un–. *Write the definition of the underlined word. Use a dictionary to check your answers.*

1. It is <u>undemocratic</u> to stop people from protesting even if you don't agree with what they're protesting about.

   definition: _____

2. Raising taxes is an <u>unpopular</u> decision that many government leaders have to make.

   definition: _____

3. Many people are <u>undecided</u> about who they are going to vote for.

   definition: _____

4. <u>Unemployment</u> is a large problem in our community. Too many people don't have jobs.

   definition: _____

You know that when you are unhappy, you're sad or not happy. What other words do you know that use *un–* as a prefix? Write them here.

_____

_____

_____

5. Suffix *–less*

The suffix *–less* means "without." You can add *–less* to some adjectives and some nouns. For example, the verb *end + less = endless*, "without end."

Complete each sentence. Use a word from the list.

homeless	hopeless	limitless	selfless	windowless

1. Mr. and Mrs. Guerra and their family do some kind of volunteer work or community service almost every month. They're the most _____ people that I know.

2. The meeting was in a dark _____ room. We had to keep the lights on all the time.

3. Tamika would like to work for the government, so she's going to go to college in Washington, DC, and study politics and civics. The opportunities there should be _____.

4. That small apartment building on King Street burned down, and now there are six _____ families. The city is trying to find places for them to live.

5. People whose lives seem _____ in their native countries often immigrate to the United States, where they hope to have a better and happier future.

Dictionaries often give spelling and definitions for words with suffixes. They may be listed with the main word or as a separate entry.

6. Compound Words

If you don't recognize a word, see if you can break it into shorter words that you do recognize. Use what you know about the shorter words to figure out the meaning.

Complete the sentences. Use words from the list.

city hall	election day	federal holidays	capital city	voting booths

1. On _____, all government offices are closed. Banks and post offices are closed, too.

2. The _____ of the United States is Washington, D.C. The people, laws, and officials that define and control the country are based there.

3. Tamra woke up early on _____ because she wanted to vote before she went to work.

4. The _____ were in the school gym.

5. Several thousand people protested in front of _____ all day. They wanted to be sure that the mayor and other government officials heard their message.

7. Context Clues: Synonyms

Look for familiar words that may be synonyms for words you don't recognize.

Read each sentence. Look for clues to help you understand the meaning of the boldfaced word. Write the meaning on the line.

1. Every four years, Americans **elect** a president. They choose a vice president, too.

   To *elect* means _____

2. Everyone has to follow the law. It's your civic responsibility to **obey** the rules of the country where you live.

   To *obey* means _____

3. The **candidate** for mayor spoke to us about crime and other problems in the city. She is one of three people who wants to be elected, so she spoke about things that were important to everyone.

   A *candidate* is _____

4. The **majority** of people in my neighborhood think we need to build a new high school. Most of us agree that the school on First Avenue is too small.

   Majority means _____

5. Every ten years, the U.S. government must take a **census**. The U.S. Census Bureau makes an official count of every person who lives in the country.

   The *census* is _____

8. Parts of Speech and the Dictionary

Some words can be nouns or verbs. A noun names a person, place, thing, or idea. A verb describes an action.

Look at each boldfaced word. What part of speech does it play? Circle noun *or* verb. *Then look up the word in a dictionary. Write the correct definition on the line.*

noun   verb   1. The government cannot **limit** the rights of its citizens.

_____

noun   verb   2. The president promised to **support** the people who lost their homes and businesses in the floods.

_____

noun   verb   3. Do you know what the **protest** at the capital was about? I heard the people were demonstrating against the plan for closing the downtown library.

_____

noun   verb   4. The **vote** for building a community center on the east side was very close.

_____

noun   verb   5. The city did a **study** to find out whether the people who live in this neighborhood are interested in building a dog park.

_____

When you look a word up in the dictionary, make sure that you are looking at the correct part of speech.

9. Multiple-Meaning Words

Some words have more than one meaning. To figure out the correct meaning, look at how the word is used in the sentence. You can also look at nearby words for clues.

Look at each underlined word. Circle the letter of the best definition.

1. The <u>bill</u> is sitting on the president's desk waiting for him to sign it.
   a. an idea for a new law that has been agreed to by the House and Senate
   b. a piece of paper money

2. The <u>cabinet</u> has been meeting all afternoon.
   a. the people who advise the president
   b. a piece of furniture with drawers or shelves for storing things

3. Rita Garza was elected to the <u>board</u> of education last month.
   a. a long, thin flat piece of wood
   b. a group of people who manage or direct something

4. Is this the <u>right</u> answer to question 6 on the civics test?
   a. a freedom
   b. correct

Unit 12 Review

Complete the paragraph. Use words from the list.

citizen	community service	free	government	limits	support

Dara is becoming a U.S. (1) _____ next month. She originally came to the United States 12 years ago because she wanted to live in a (2) _____ country where she felt there were no (3) _____. To celebrate her new life, she's going to perform (4) _____ at the senior center. She wants to thank the neighbors and friends who (5) _____ her and help the (6) _____ of the country that welcomes her.

Complete the chart. Use words from the list.

democracy	demonstrate	responsibilities	rights	taxes	vote

Describing U.S. (7) _____	
(8) _____	**(9)** _____
• (10) _____ in public for or against something that is important to you.	• Respect and follow the law.
• Say what you believe	• (11) Pay _____.
• (12) _____ in elections.	• Participate in the community.

Read each question. Then circle the correct answer.

1. **What does the word *free* mean in this passage?**

   You can say whatever you want to say when you speak in public. You're <u>free</u> to speak about anything that's important to you. But you can't yell "Fire!" in a crowded building because that is a dangerous action.

   A not busy

   B costing nothing

   C not occupied

   D not controlled by other people

2. **Which choice makes sense in the passage?**

   Many states offer early voting to give people more time to vote. But many people still choose to vote on _____.

   A community service

   B election day

   C city hall

   D polling place

3. **Which of these words means "without control"?**

   A powerless

   B powered

   C powerful

   D powered

4. **Which choice means about the same as *majority* in the sentence below?**

   A <u>majority</u> of the voters voted to ban smoking in the town's restaurants.

   A most

   B few

   C all

   D none

5. **What does the word *demonstrate* mean in this sentence?**

   The students are going to <u>demonstrate</u> against raising the cost of classes.

   A to show how to do something

   B to show you have an ability

   C to prove

   D to publicly complain against something

6. **Which word or words from the passage mean about the same as *right*?**

   Mr. Lorenz opened the letter from the government immediately. It was a census form. He wanted to fill the form out <u>right</u>, so first he read it all the way from top to bottom. He was happy because he knew all of his answers were correct. Completing the census form is a freedom Mr. Lorenz enjoyed.

   A immediately

   B all the way

   C correctly

   D freedom

7. **Which choice is an example of a *right*?**

   A vetoing a bill

   B taking the census

   C voting

   D paying taxes

8. **Which of these words means "not done"?**

   A redone

   B undone

   C overdone

   D outdone

How are a child's rights and responsibilities different from those of an adult? Write your answer on a separate sheet of paper. In your answer, use at least six words you learned in this unit. Circle the vocabulary words you use.

Check your answers on page 108.

Answer Key

UNIT 1

Exercise 1, p. 9

1.	e	7.	j
2.	h	8.	c
3.	b	9.	l
4.	i	10.	k
5.	d	11.	a
6.	g	12.	f

Exercise 4, p. 11

Definitions will vary.

Exercise 5, p. 11

1. successful
2. meaningful
3. stressful
4. peaceful

Exercise 6, p. 12

1. brainstorm
2. online classes
3. checklist
4. full-time
5. study group

Exercise 7, p. 12

Definitions will vary.

Exercise 8, p. 13

1. verb
2. noun
3. verb
4. verb

Definitions will vary.

Exercise 9, p. 13

1.	a	3.	a
2.	b	4.	a

Review, p. 14

1. balance
2. counselor
3. stress
4. active
5. commitment

6. succeed
7. resource
8. focus
9. participate
10. opinion
11. connect
12. reasonable

Review, p. 15

1.	A	5.	A
2.	C	6.	A
3.	C	7.	B
4.	D	8.	B

UNIT 2

Exercise 1, p. 17

1.	k	7.	g
2.	e	8.	b
3.	j	9.	f
4.	h	10.	d
5.	l	11.	i
6.	a	12.	c

Exercise 4, p. 19

1. misunderstood
2. miscounted
3. misused
4. misspelled
5. misplaced
6. misjudged

Exercise 5, p. 19

1.	e	4.	a
2.	d	5.	c
3.	f	6.	b

Exercise 6, p. 20

1. people skills
2. feedback
3. Teamwork
4. public speaking

Exercise 7, p. 20

Definitions will vary.

Exercise 8, p. 21

Definitions will vary.

Exercise 9, p. 21

1.	b	4.	a
2.	a	5.	b
3.	a		

Review, p. 22

1. research
2. improve
3. key
4. skills
5. effective
6. react
7. perspectives
8. Communication
9. appreciate
10. confident
11. message
12. listener
13. cooperate
14. feedback

Review, p. 23

1.	D	5.	A
2.	C	6.	A
3.	A	7.	C
4.	D	8.	B

UNIT 3

Exercise 1, p. 25

1. location
2. owner
3. utilities
4. roommate
5. affordable
6. damage
7. repair
8. neighborhood
9. apartment
10. deposit
11. lease

12. mortgage

Exercise 4, p. 27

1. repay
2. repaint
3. review
4. replace
5. rebuild

Exercise 5, p. 27

1. available
2. dependable
3. affordable
4. comfortable
5. noticeable

Exercise 6, p. 28

1. living room
2. newspaper
3. building manager
4. apartment building
5. roommates
6. bedroom

Exercise 7, p. 28

1. owner
2. renters
3. spots on the carpet, holes in the walls
4. rent, utilities, food
5. buy
6. sofa, table, chairs

Exercise 8, p. 29

1.	b	4.	b
2.	c	5.	a
3.	a		

6.–7. Definitions will vary.

Review, p. 30

1. affordable
2. newspaper
3. roommate
4. bedrooms

5. location
6. available
7. comfortable
8. apartment building
9. repairs
10. building manager
11. research
12. purchase
13. mortgage
14. repay
15. expenses
16. furniture

Review, p. 31
1. C 5. B
2. B 6. C
3. D 7. D
4. A 8. D

UNIT 4

Exercise 1, p. 33
1. transportation
2. fare
3. commute
4. urban
5. distance
6. toll
7. insurance
8. public
9. route
10. traffic
11. maintenance
12. schedule

Exercise 4, p. 35
1. transfer
2. translate
3. transit
4. transparent
5. transport

Exercise 5, p. 35
1. locally
2. exactly
3. usually
4. frequently

5. easily
6. quickly

Exercise 6, p. 36
1. sidewalk
2. traffic light
3. parking lot
4. bike lane
5. speed limit
6. highway
7. bus stop
8. underground
9. crosswalk
10. taxi driver

Exercise 7, p. 36
1. riders
2. crash
3. cars
4. stay home
5. arrives
6. drivers

Exercise 8, p. 37
Definitions will vary.

Exercise 9, p. 37
1. a 3. b
2. b 4. b

Review, p. 38
1. traffic
2. parking lot
3. transportation
4. frequently
5. routes
6. station
7. fare
8. pedestrians
9. sidewalks
10. traffic light
11. quickly
12. vehicle
13. accident
14. carefully
15. passenger
16. insurance

Review, p. 39
1. C 5. B
2. D 6. D
3. B 7. C
4. D 8. A

UNIT 5

Exercise 1, p. 41
1. detail
2. routine
3. lead
4. career
5. organize
6. training
7. networking
8. control
9. employment
10. search
11. apply
12. decrease

Exercise 4, p. 43
1. d 4. a
2. e 5. c
3. b

Exercise 5, p. 43
1. applying
2. looking
3. making
4. stopping
5. taking
6. training
7. Taking
8. making
9. applying
10. stopping
11. training
12. looking

Exercise 6, p. 44
1. job application
2. workshop
3. full-time
4. paperwork
5. job fair

6. background

Exercise 7, p. 44
Definitions will vary.

Exercise 8, p. 45
1. verb 3. noun
2. verb 4. verb
Definitions will vary.

Exercise 9, p. 45
1. b 4. a
2. a 5. b
3. b

Review, p. 46
1. apply
2. training
3. leads
4. search
5. organize
6. networking
7. career
8. control
9. routine
10. decrease
11. employment
12. details

Review, p. 47
1. A 5. B
2. B 6. C
3. C 7. A
4. C 8. C

UNIT 6

Exercise 1, p. 49
1. interest
2. balance
3. account
4. service
5. electronically
6. minimum
7. withdraw
8. automatically
9. deposit
10. fee

11. debit card
12. manage

Exercise 4, p. 51
Sentences will vary.

Exercise 5, p. 51
1. financial
2. central
3. approval
4. withdrawal
5. educational

Exercise 6, p. 52
1. c   5. f
2. g   6. b
3. d   7. e
4. a

Exercise 7, p. 52
1. a   3. a
2. b   4. b

Exercise 8, p. 53
1. verb
2. verb
3. noun
4. noun
5. noun
6. verb
Definitions will vary.

Exercise 9, p. 53
1. b   3. b
2. a   4. b

Review, p. 54
1. overtime
2. overworked
3. paycheck
4. additional
5. financial
6. overspent
7. balance
8. account
9. bounced
10. fee

11. payday
12. deposit
13. security guard
14. deposit slip
15. teller
16. direct deposit
17. automatically

Review, p. 55
1. D   5. B
2. B   6. A
3. B   7. C
4. A   8. D

UNIT 7

Exercise 1, p. 57
1. f   7. d
2. i   8. e
3. a   9. c
4. k   10. g
5. b   11. h
6. l   12. j

Exercise 4, p. 59
Definitions will vary.

Exercise 5, p. 59
1. statement
2. agreement
3. employment
4. advertisement
5. payment
6. shipment

Exercise 6, p. 60
1. checkout line
2. sales tax
3. clearance sale
4. checkbook
5. salesperson
6. downtown
7. barcode
8. online shopping

Exercise 7, p. 60
Definitions will vary.

Exercise 8, p. 61
1. verb   4. noun
2. verb   5. noun
3. verb
Definitions will vary.

Exercise 9, p. 61
1. a   3. a
2. b   4. b

Review, p. 62
1. online shopping
2. convenient
3. checkout lines
4. credit card
5. purchases
6. advertisement
7. clearance sale
8. salesperson
9. discount
10. receipt
11. exchange
12. self-checkout
13. scan
14. insert
15. cashier

Review, p. 63
1. C   5. B
2. B   6. C
3. C   7. D
4. D   8. C

UNIT 8

Exercise 1, p. 65
1. diagnose
2. prevent
3. annual
4. copayment
5. symptom
6. examine
7. appointment
8. specialist
9. prescription
10. medical

11. complicated
12. disease

Exercise 4, p. 67
1. disagree
2. disturb
3. discovered
4. disease
5. disabled

Exercise 5, p. 67
1. vision
2. vaccinations
3. confusion
4. medication
5. operation
6. examination
7. suggestions
8. infection

Exercise 6, p. 68
1. eye doctor
2. checkup
3. office visit
4. drugstore
5. headache

Exercise 7, p. 68
1. get seven hours of sleep per night; lose some weight
2. a cut, a broken bone, and a bruise
3. get medication his doctor prescribed
4. heart, lung, stomach
5. breathing problems, heart disease
6. heart disease; diabetes
Definitions will vary.

Exercise 8, p. 69
Definitions will vary.

Exercise 9, p. 69
Definitions will vary.

Review, p. 70

1. appointment
2. symptoms
3. vision
4. headaches
5. examination
6. infection
7. prescribe
8. pharmacy
9. prevent
10. Vaccination
11. shot
12. complications
13. conditions
14. prescription
15. treat
16. recommendations
17. medical

Review, p. 71

1. B
2. D
3. A
4. D
5. C
6. A
7. D
8. C

UNIT 9

Exercise 1, p. 73

1. produce
2. impulse
3. label
4. aisle
5. packaged
6. items
7. experts
8. perimeter
9. facts
10. nutritionists
11. processed
12. ingredient

Exercise 4, p. 75

1. e
2. c
3. d
4. b
5. a

Exercise 5, p. 75

1. bigger
2. closer
3. fresher
4. healthier
5. hungrier
6. hungrier
7. healthier
8. bigger
9. closer
10. fresher

Exercise 6, p. 76

1. expiration date
2. whole grain
3. bulk food
4. farmers' market
5. shopping carts
6. weekly specials
7. store brands

Exercise 7, p. 76

Definitions will vary.

Exercise 8, p. 77

Definitions will vary.

Exercise 9, p. 77

1. b
2. b
3. b
4. a
5. b

Review, p. 78

1. nutritionists
2. packaged
3. labels
4. ingredients
5. produce
6. facts
7. aisles
8. Experts
9. items
10. processed
11. impulse
12. perimeter

Review, p. 79

1. A
2. C
3. C
4. B
5. C
6. D
7. C
8. B

UNIT 10

Exercise 1, p. 81

1. crime
2. password
3. message
4. online
5. multiple
6. laptop
7. acccss
8. identity theft
9. email
10. character
11. data
12. protect

Exercise 4, p. 83

Sentences will vary.

Exercise 5, p. 83

1. portable
2. transportation
3. imported
4. support
5. report
6. portfolio

Exercise 6, p. 84

1. keyboard
2. download
3. user name
4. smartphone
5. search engine

Exercise 7, p. 84

1. vulnerable
2. attachment
3. security
4. socialize
5. blog
6. monitor

Exercise 8, p. 85

Definitions will vary.

Exercise 9, p. 85

1. a
2. b
3. b
4. b
5. a

Review, p. 86

1. online
2. reports
3. laptop
4. blogs
5. keyboard
6. smartphone
7. socialize
8. encourage
9. contact
10. enforcing
11. password
12. email
13. messages
14. monitor
15. download
16. viruses
17. data

Review, p. 87

1. D
2. D
3. A
4. B
5. D
6. A
7. C
8. C

UNIT 11

Exercise 1, p. 89

1. print
2. broadcast
3. inform
4. article
5. section
6. current
7. local
8. mass media
9. reporter
10. cable

11. entertain
12. issue

Exercise 4, p. 91
1. vision
2. television
3. video
4. revise
5. visible
6. supervises

Exercise 5, p. 91
Sentences will vary.

Exercise 6, p. 92
1. TV station
2. advice column
3. byline
4. press conference
5. headline

Exercise 7, p. 92
Definitions will vary.

Exercise 8, p. 93
1. noun
2. verb
3. adjective
4. verb
5. noun
6. verb
7. adjective
8. noun

Exercise 9, p. 93
1. b   4. b
2. a   5. a
3. a

Review, p. 94
1. subscribe
2. local
3. current
4. articles
5. headlines
6. advice column
7. section
8. skims
9. stories
10. column
11. columnist
12. television
13. video
14. cable
15. channel
16. forecast

Review, p. 95
1. D   5. A
2. B   6. D
3. A   7. A
4. C   8. D

UNIT 12

Exercise 1, p. 97
1. f   7. b
2. k   8. i
3. h   9. e
4. g   10. l
5. j   11. a
6. d   12. c

Exercise 4, p. 99
Definitions will vary.

Exercise 5, p. 99
1. selfless
2. windowless
3. limitless
4. homeless
5. hopeless

Exercise 6, p. 100
1. federal holidays
2. capital city
3. election day
4. voting booths
5. city hall

Exercise 7, p. 100
Definitions will vary.

Exercise 8, p. 101
1. verb   4. noun
2. verb   5. noun
3. noun
Definitions will vary.

Exercise 9, p. 101
1. a   3. b
2. a   4. b

Review, p. 102
1. citizen
2. free
3. limits
4. community service
5. support
6. government
7. Democracy
8. Rights
9. Responsibilities
10. Demonstrate
11. taxes
12. Vote

Review, p. 103
1. D   5. D
2. B   6. C
3. A   7. C
4. A   8. B

Appendix I: Common Prefixes

Prefix	Meaning	Example
anti–	against	antibiotic
de–	opposite, down	decrease
dis–	not, opposite of	disagree
em– en–	cause to	employ encode
fore–	before	foresee
il– in– im– ir–	not, opposite of	illegal indirect impossible irresponsible
in– im–	in or into	invite immigrate
inter–	among, between	interpersonal
mid–	middle	midterm
mis–	wrongly	misspeak
non–	not, opposite of	nonsense
over–	too much, above	overdo
pre–	before	presell
re–	again, back	retell
semi–	half	semicircle
sub–	under, lower	subtitle
super	above, beyond	supermarket
un–	not, opposite of	unhappy
under–	too little, below	underrated underground

Appendix II: Common Suffixes

Suffix	Meaning	Example
–able, –ible	is, can be	comfortable
–al, –ial	having characteristics of	personal
–ed	past form of verbs	wanted
–en	made of	wooden
–er	comparative	longer
–er –or	one who	teacher inventor
–est	superlative	deepest
–ful	full of	careful
–ic	having characteristics of	scientific
–ing	verb form—present participle	speaking
–ion –tion –ation –ition	act, process	occasion introduction decoration definition
–ist	one who practices	nutritionist
–ity –y	state of	activity infinity
–ive –ative –itive	adjective form of a noun	decisive informative repetitive
–less	without	fearless
–ly	characteristic of	happily
–ment	action or process	employment
–ness	state of, condition of	goodness
–ous –eous –ious	possessing the qualities of	dangerous righteous serious
–s –es	plural	books boxes
–y	characterized by	funny

Appendix III: Common Roots

Root	Meaning	Example
audi	hear	audience
auto	self	automobile
bio	life	biology
cycle	wheel, circle	bicycle recycle
dic dict	say, speak	dictate predict
duc duct	make, lead	produce conduct
geo	earth	geography
graph	write	biography
jur jus	law	jury justice
logy	study of	biology
mand mend	order	command recommend
meter metr	measure	perimeter geometry
multi	many	multipurpose
phon	sound	telephone
port	carry	portable
scrib script	write	scribble prescription
tele	far off	television
therm	heat	thermometer
trans	across, change	transport transform
vid vis	see	video vision

Personal Dictionary

Create your own dictionary. Write down any words you want to remember.

Word	Definition	Used in a Sentence	Notes